HOMEWORKS®

A New American Townhouse

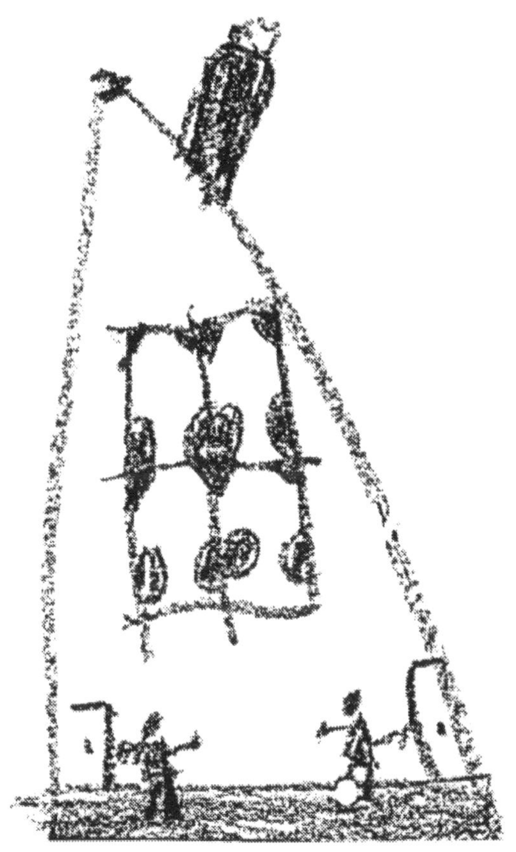

Stephen Kendall, PhD

Director, Building Futures Institute
Ball State University

July 2006

Book layout and design: Sabreena Shrestha, Sujata Tuladhar
Printed by: Digitalisbooks

Professor of Architecture
Director, Building Futures Institute
Ball State University

Note for Librarians: A cataloguing record for this book is available from Library and Archives Canada at www.collectionscanada.ca/amicus/index-e.html
ISBN 1-4120-9424-0

Offices in Canada, USA, Ireland and UK

Book sales for North America and international:
Trafford Publishing, 6E–2333 Government St.,
Victoria, BC V8T 4P4 CANADA
phone 250 383 6864 (toll-free 1 888 232 4444)
fax 250 383 6804; email to orders@trafford.com
Book sales in Europe:
Trafford Publishing (UK) Limited, 9 Park End Street, 2nd Floor
Oxford, UK OX1 1HH UNITED KINGDOM
phone +44 (0)1865 722 113 (local rate 0845 230 9601)
facsimile +44 (0)1865 722 868; info.uk@trafford.com
Order online at:
trafford.com/06-1179

10 9 8 7 6

Contents

Preface

Townhouse Living by HOMEWORKS® 1

Chapter 1 Introduction to HOMEWORKS 2
A New Approach 2
Managing Variety 3
A New Delivery Process 3
Taking Initiative 7
Decision Flow 9

Chapter 2 **HOMEWORKS® delivers solutions** 10
INFILL "KITS" 10
Quality control through multi-skilled work teams 11
Opportunities for mass-customization and product innovation 12
Long-term stock adaptability 12

Chapter 3 **HOMEWORKS® Principles** 13

Chapter 4 **HOMEWORKS® assumptions** 24
Ordinary products 24
Some new processes required 24
Existing CAD and data software can be modified 24
New business formation 24
Task Partitioning 25
Scope of Work 26
Technical Interfaces 26
The Regulatory Environment 26

Chapter 5 Problems in conventional townhouse developments 28
Process rigidity and inability to respond to market "pull" 28
Technical and organizational entanglement 28
Obstruction of innovation and manufacturing "push" 29
Excessive waste in materials and labor 29

Conclusion 30

Appendix 1 Untangling the American House 32

Appendix 2 Where to get more information 46

Appendix 3 Notes on Attribution and Sources 48

PREFACE

HOMEWORKS offers technical solutions, strategies, logistics and methods in support of a new way of building townhouses in the "woodframe" tradition.

But all of this is only interesting if we first recognize that the current state of the housing stock is degrading in its repetitiveness, stunningly inattentive to individuals, riddled by poor quality and incapable of long-term adaptability. The current methods of house building are not only detrimental to the building stock per se as a public/private asset, thus passing on a massive economic and environmental burden to our children. They are demeaning to its inhabitants – all of us - and to the people building the houses.

Our challenge is therefore not only technical. It is fundamentally to reengage people with their living environments while also finding a way that will lead to more decent, dignified and caring professions in the building arts. Today, these two HUMAN issues cannot be addressed by the way we build.

The reason I wrote HOMEWORKS is to see it implemented. That being said, this monograph is largely a book of principles. Its applications will take varied forms and use varied technologies. But to be implemented, investment is needed and risks assumed. HOMEWORKS constitutes a very big change in practices and habits, and requires clear-headed technical thinking to avoid the inevitable traps facing any innovation in the housing industry, much less one as comprehensive as this. A number of technical issues still must be solved. A target market must be identified. Assurance of financial stability must be given to the team in charge of implementing HOMEWORKS. So this is written with no illusions.

In spite of the resistance - on both ideological and practical grounds - I believe the time is right for such an alternative to be taken seriously.

Much has been learned in the application of open building principles to multi-unit housing over the past 30 years around the world. Commercial development is now happening in Japan, Finland, Russia, Switzerland and the Netherlands, and probably elsewhere.

But too little progress has been made toward the adoption of open building methods in the dominantly wooden house building tradition.

I offer HOMEWORKS as part of the ongoing effort in which many are engaged, to reform the way we build that sprang to life in the US in Chicago in first part of the 19th century. While not rejecting much that this tradition offers, HOMEWORKS takes what I believe to be a necessary next step in the evolution of our venerable "2x4" system.

Townhouse Living by HOMEWORKS®

The new HOMEWORKS townhouses in Clear Creek feature a totally new way for buyers to get what they want in a "new urbanist" development north of the city.

What's unique about the development is that HOMEWORKS offers a large menu of interior floor plan layouts, equipment and finish packages that can be installed in any of the units in the development. If you like a unit closer to the park, facing east, you can select from a wide array of floor plans. If you like a unit in the middle of a row with the back yard facing south, you can also select from the same array of choices in interior layout. If you have an elderly parent moving in with you, or if you are a young couple expecting children, there is also a range of layouts just for you. Because of the sophisticated construction method, each layout and equipment design on a given floor can be chosen largely independent of the other floors in the townhouse, so the choices are very large. Whats more, because of the way HOMEWORKS houses are built, the interior you choose now can be altered later to a large extent.

All menu selections include state-of-the-art cabinet, finish and equipment choices, backed up by the latest energy efficiency methods. For example, if you want a large open kitchen next to the family room, you can have that. Or, you can have a formal dining room separated from the living room and kitchen. These are only some of the choices.

This is possible because of a totally new approach to marketing and construction. The developer has obtained approval for construction, but has not yet made decisions about what goes inside each unit. This is for you to decide. Each unit is designed to accommodate whatever interior package you want. You can even get a fully customized design. HOMEWORKS provides the kit to fill in your preferred unit, just-in-time and to the exact specs you have selected and at the exact price and schedule that suits your family.

Many advanced industries are offering what HOMEWORKS now offers for the first time in residential construction – "mass customization". This idea brings together the efficiencies of factory production and quality control with a fully organized menu of choices from which to compose your own house. The choices on the exterior are more limited but the choices in the interior are astounding.

The model townhouse at Clear Creek has a showroom that allows prospective buyers to use advanced computer visualization tools and cost estimating software to quickly "build" a virtual model of the unit, take a virtual walk-through and get immediate cost information. The computer then allows the buyer to modify the plan, equipment, finishes, cabinets and so on and get immediate costs. The drawings can be printed out, and the buyer can go home and discuss the plans around the dining table. This process can be repeated several times until the buyer is happy, a contract is signed, and six weeks later they can move into their customized unit.

Soon, HOMEWORKS® will be announcing another development, this one supported by a web-based menu selection and design process, where you can work on alternative layout ideas in the comfort of your own home before going to the showroom to make final decisions.

(A fictitious article in a major metropolitan area's Real Estate section of the newspaper)

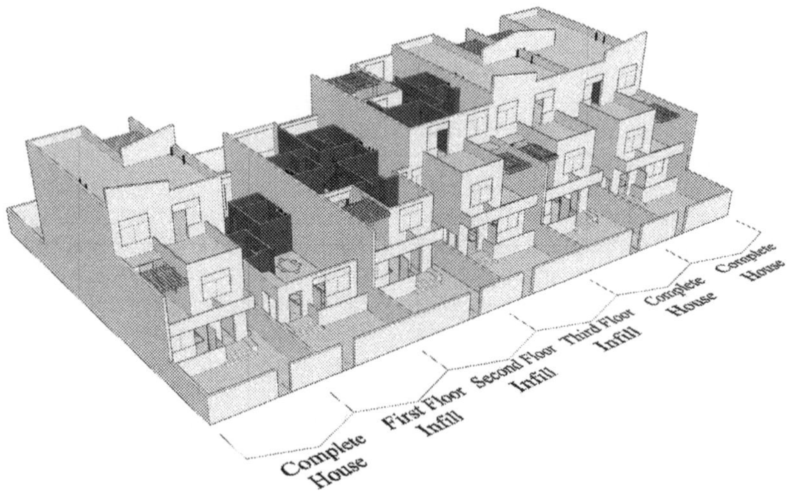

Figure 1: Image of INFILL on each floor of an hypothetical HOMEWORKS® development

A New Approach

HOMEWORKS® is a new approach to the design and construction of townhouses. The approach has two primary objectives:

1) to reduce the risk to developers in delivering for-sale houses that meet individual consumer preferences, and,

2) to produce buildings that are less costly and wasteful to adapt over the long term.

The approach calls for a strict separation between the part of the house that should have a long life, and the part of the house that can be customized initially and adapt over time in response to changing household preferences and upgrades in consumer-oriented technologies.

These two parts are called the "SHELL" and the "INFILL".

The "SHELL" constitutes the technical components and spaces that are likely to have the longest life. These include foundations, building structure and enclosure, the main MEP (mechanical, electrical and plumbing) and installation systems risers and laterals, and their connection to the public portion of these utility systems. The stairway position is also part of the SHELL. These are the parts about which local regulation is most concerned and which are most tightly interdependant with adjacent house designs.

The "INFILL" constitutes the technical components that are most subject to individual household preferences, both initially and over time. These include the interior non-load-bearing partitions, the stairs, floor finishes, cabinets and casework, fixtures, and the MEP systems directly associated with the arrangement of "INFILL" components. These are the parts that can be selected or altered without effecting adjacent town-houses.

Once the SHELL and INFILL are distinguished, their combination allows a wide array of choices for buyers, and better control of these choices by the developer. It should be possible to install a variety of INFILL layouts and products in a given SHELL.

The principle technical strategy of HOMEWORKS® is to avoid burying consumer-sensitive wiring and plumbing inside the SHELL walls and floors. As much of the cabling and piping as possible should therefore be part of the INFILL.

The principle logistical strategy of HOMEWORKS® is the use of "kitting" or product bundling particularly of the "INFILL", and the employment of "work cell" teams to install the kits, replacing the normal sequencing of subcontractors.

Managing Variety

Instead of delivering a unified product – a "whole" townhouse - in which all decisions and products are interdependent, it is possible to deliver SHELL and INFILL as separate "products". This helps everyone, because each product responds to a different set of performance requirements, can take advantage of a variety of financing instruments and production processes, and corresponds to distinct decision-making processes and markets.

The reason to do this is to manage variation and enable decision flexibility with reduced risk. The SHELL follows a decision path that depends heavily on public approvals and is sensitive to large-scale development decisions. The INFILL follows a decision sequence that is as independent as possible of the approval of local public authorities, while meeting public health, safety and welfare requirements through "systems" approvals of such bodies as the Underwriters Laboratory. The INFILL is also designed to enable decisions about each dwelling unit's interior layout, finishes and equipment to be separated from site-planning decisions and later changed without requiring a change to the SHELL.

A New Delivery Process

HOMEWORKS® requires a new delivery process that accounts for the distinction between a SHELL and an INFILL kit. This can be seen in the following diagrams. In each, the basic element groups are shown comprising the INFILL:

a. Stair
b. INFILL walls
c. Kitchen and bathroom equipment and specific MEP lines associated with these elements

The SHELL – including window and other façade elements and fixed MEP system parts – and the Furniture are also shown in the diagrams on the following pages.

The diagrams show three different delivery processes: a conventional process, a modified conventional and what is called a "maximum buyer choice" process, the latter being HOMEWORKS®. In each diagram, decisions are indicated as being made either by the developer or the occupant or homebuyer.

Conventional Process

In a conventional house delivery process, the developer has unified control of all the parts making the house, but still depends on multiple subcontractors each of which brings materials to the site and is responsible for installing them. Quality assurance is difficult as is control of schedule and price. In the conventional process, the household's primary choice lies in the furnishings and a few other minor variations. (Figure 2)

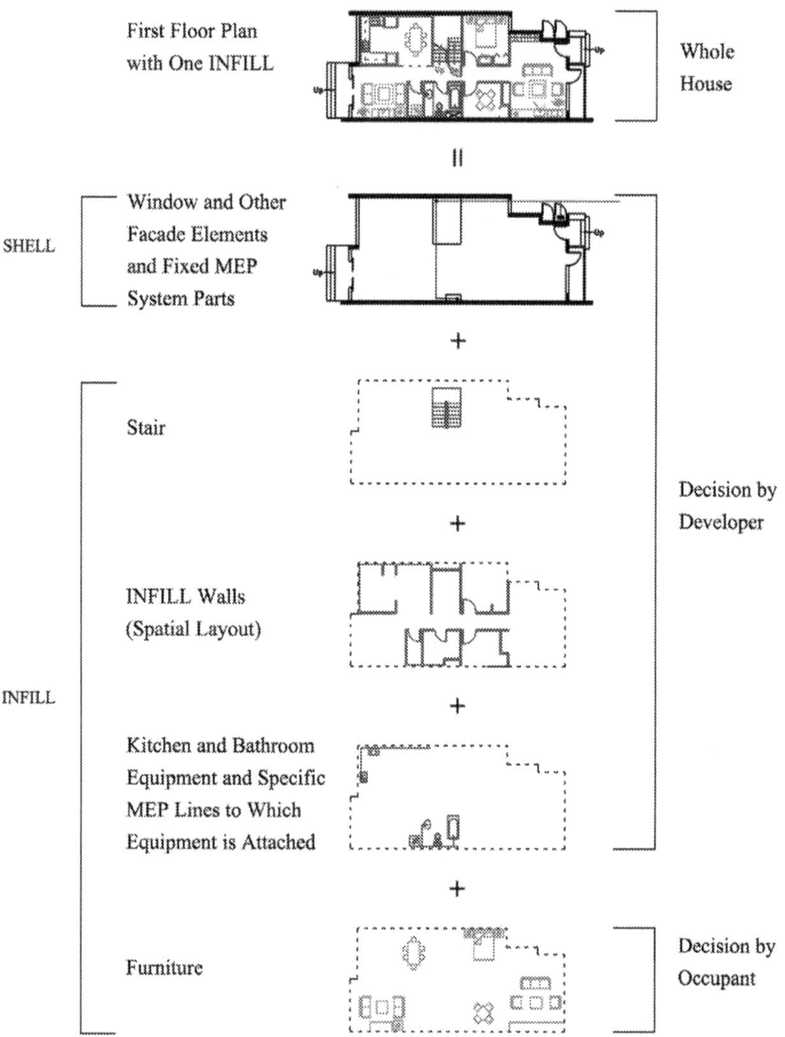

Figure 2: Conventional Decision Process

Modified Process

Some developers, targeting the market where households are willing to pay for choice, organize their delivery process a little differently, providing a wider measure of choice. In this process, the developer has a more complex process to manage, having to negotiate prices and quality with the buyer, the contractor and the subcontractors. Potential conflicts arise when buyers want wider choice, the subcontractors charge more, and the contractor raises the price of construction to cover his risk and management complexity. Many variations on this "modified" process exist, with the emphasis on expanding choice while managing price and risk. (Figure 3)

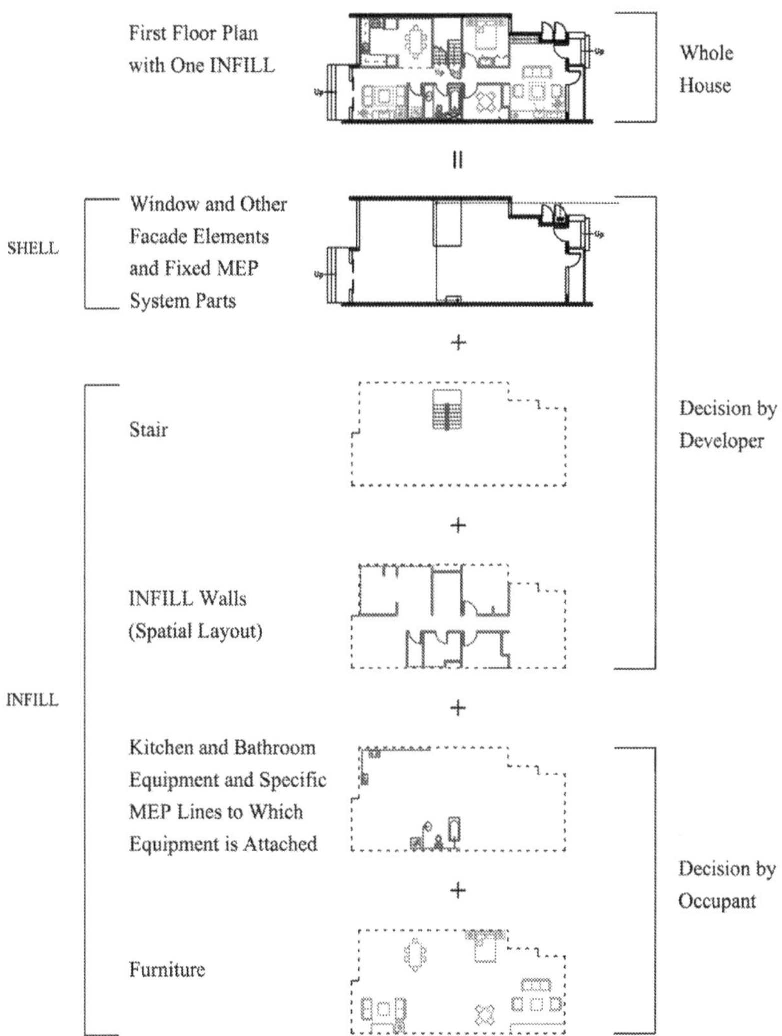

Figure 3: Modified Decision Process

HOMEWORKS® Process

HOMEWORKS® suggests a significant, but still incremental enlargement of the decisions available to the household. (Figure 4) Generally, with conventional delivery methods, enlarging choice raises the level of risk to the developer and heightens the likelihood of conflict, because offering more choice and variation always presents difficulties and uncertainties. What follows is an explanation of one way to solve these problems facing the developer operating in this third model, and suggests how it can be beneficial to the developer, the contractor and the buyer.

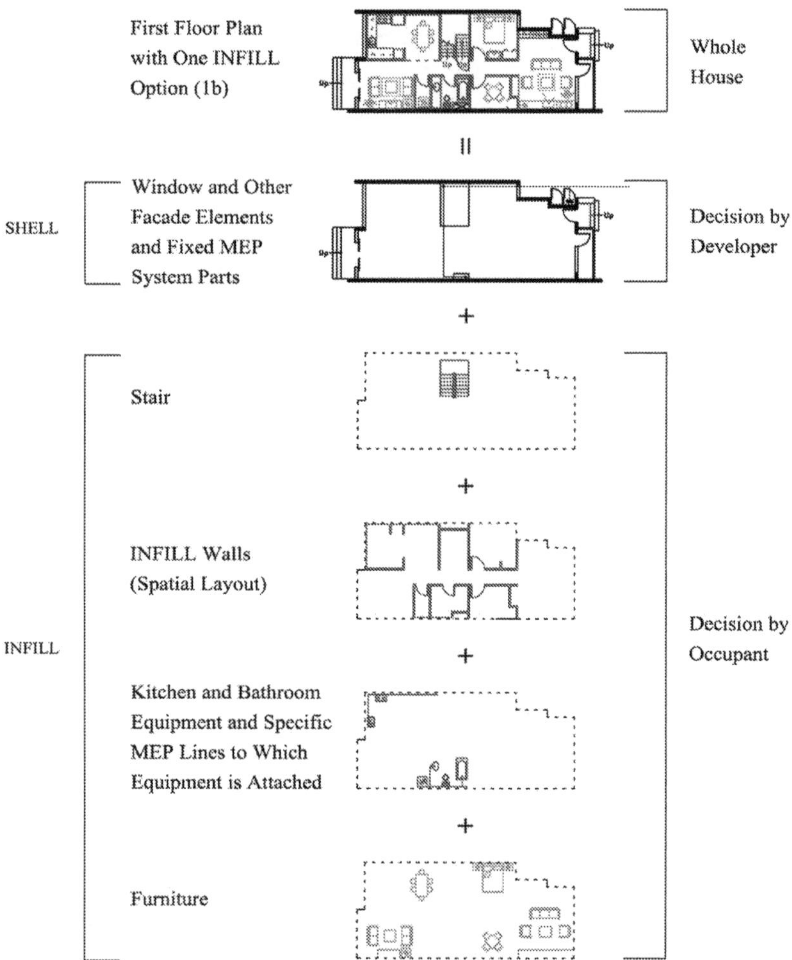

Figure 4: Maximum Buyer Choice

Taking Initiative

Given a fixed SHELL and variable INFILL, several choices are available in meeting market demand. The following diagrams describe some of these choices.

Initiative by a Developer

First, consider that a developer's construction division builds SHELLS ready for INFILL, on a speculative basis, based on market demand analysis. This can be organised in several ways. (Figure 5: 1, 2, 3)

In the first case, the contractor can build the SHELL, and the homebuyer then purchases the SHELL and at the same time the homebuyer signs a contract with a separate INFILL contractor to fill in the SHELL.

In the second case, the contractor builds the SHELL, the homebuyer purchases it, and the homebuyer contracts with the INFILL division of the construction company that built the SHELL, to provide the INFILL.

In the third case, the contractor builds the SHELL, the homebuyer purchases it, and the contractor that built the SHELL subcontracts with a separate INFILL contractor to provide the INFILL selected by the homebuyer.

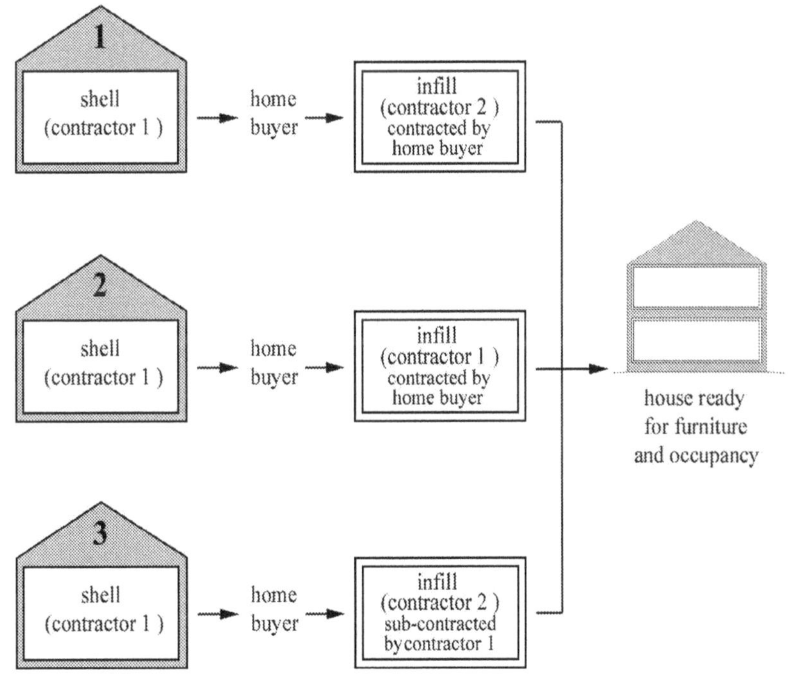

Figure 5: Contractor Initiative

Initiative by the Homebuyer

Homebuyers can also take the initiative. (Figure 6: 1, 2, 3)

In the first case, the homebuyer looks for a development company who can build SHELLs. The developer's SHELL construction division has a menu of SHELL choices from which the homebuyer chooses. The same construction company also has an INFILL division and the homebuyer selects from that INFILL division the right INFILL for price, quality and delivery schedule.

In the second case, the homebuyer also looks for a development company who can build a SHELL the homebuyer likes, from a menu of SHELL choices. In this case the homeowner goes to an independent INFILL producer and selects the preferred INFILL, signs a contract and the INFILL provider installs the INFILL.

In the third case, the homebuyer hires an architect directly and a contractor is hired to build the SHELL. In this case, the homebuyer goes to an INFILL provider, selects the preferred INFILL and installs it by their own labor.

Other combinations are possible, but these variations in initiative and responsibilities illustrate the main principle.

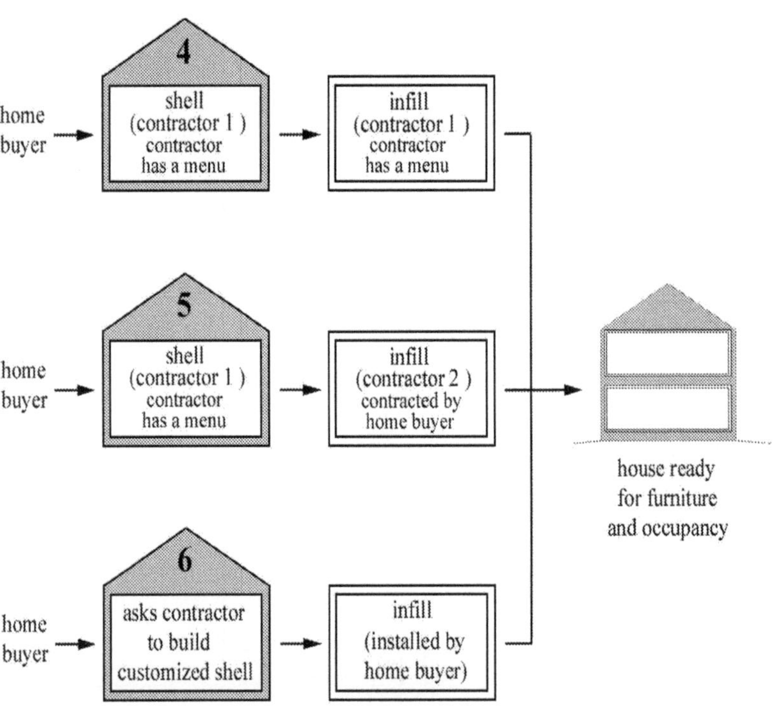

Figure 6: Homeowner Initiative

Decision Sequence

The seperation of a SHELL process from an INFILL process offers a way to control variety but also raises new issues of coordination, somewhat different from conventional process management. These issues are addressed later. But this requires adjustments to normal decision making procedures and habits.

The following diagram represents the principle decision points in a HOMEWORKS® house delivery. (Figure 7)

To implement these principles, decision-making for a HOMEWORKS® townhouse is organized hierarchically. Decisions follow a certain order in a "decision tree" once a specific site has been selected for a HOMEWORKS® townhouse development. While this diagram represents the principle approach, the precise distribution of responsibilities, regulatory approvals, and scheduling will vary in each locale.

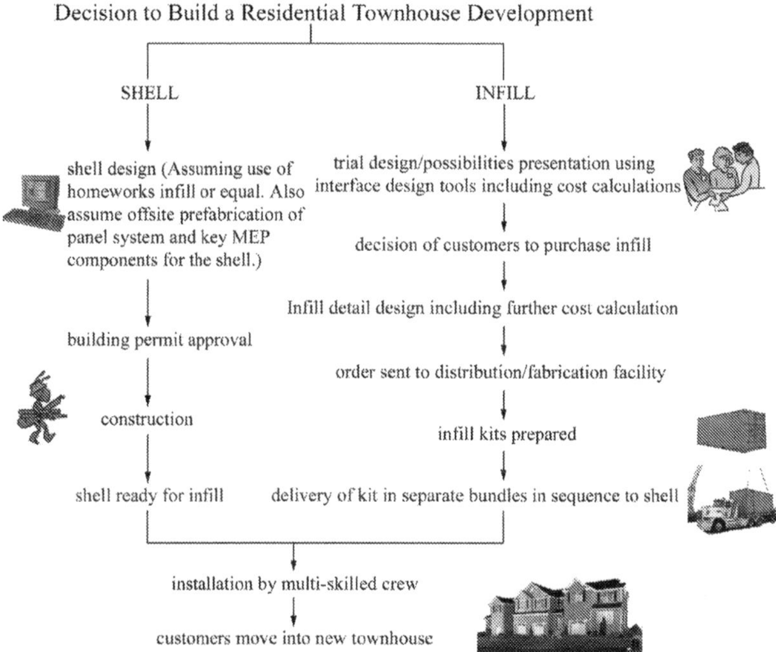

Figure 7: Decision Sequence Diagram

Summary

Chapter One has presented the organizational concept of HOMEWORKS®. Chapter 2 describes in broad terms what solutions HOMEWORKS® delivers. Chapter 3 discusses HOMEWORKS® technical principles. Chapter 4 outlines basic assumptions. This new approach responds to a number of problems in conventional townhouse development practices, discussed in Chapter 5. Appendix 1 is an essay first written in 1994, originally titled "The Entangled American House", and Appendix 2 offers other sources of information related to this monograph.

HOMEWORKS® delivers solutions by introducing a sharp technical and organizational distinction between a serviced SHELL and the INFILL that fills in the empty space in the shell. Because of this separation, the infill can be customized for each occupant / homebuyer, or can be selected by the developer with virtually no additional management costs. This is possible because the INFILL is systematically prepared in the form of INFILL "KITS".

INFILL "KITS"

INFILL "KITS" (or product bundles) are the key to HOMEWORKS® new process. An INFILL kit includes all the parts needed to fill in an empty SHELL space to make it habitable. The precise specification of parts included in an INFILL KIT will vary from one provider to another, and from one "building technology" to another. For example, in a SHELL built with precast concrete panels, the INFILL may include not only the interior parts, but also the façade or "cladding". In other cases, the INFILL may include the interior finishes of the SHELL exterior walls.

In general, an INFILL KIT for townhouses includes the following basic element groups:

<u>Interior walls</u>
Metal studs, drywall, doorframes, doors and hardware, misc. hardware, etc.

<u>Stairs</u>
Risers and treads, stringers, bannister, trim package, etc.

<u>Cabinets</u>
Kitchen and bathroom cabinets, etc.

<u>Fixtures and Equipment</u>
Tub, shower, toilets, sinks, dishwasher, lighting fixtures, etc.

<u>Mechanical</u>
HVAC unit, water heater(s), ductwork or pipes, bathroom and kitchen exhaust fans/ducts, etc.

<u>Plumbing</u>
Hot and cold-water piping, fittings, drain lines and fittings, fasteners, gas lines, etc.

<u>Electrical and Signal</u>
Circuit breakers, home network panel, power and data cabling, boxes, terminations, etc.

<u>Finishes</u>
Floor finishes, tile, trim, etc.

Ideally, all the parts making an individual INFILL KIT are prepared in an off-site production facility set up for this kind of production, with jig tables, racks, and other production equipment. The parts are then loaded into containers or trucks in reverse order of their installation sequence, delivered to the site and installed by multi-skilled installation teams or "work cells". All parts are small enough to be brought in through SHELL doors or windows.

The following diagram (Figure 8), used to describe an integrated INFILL system developed and used in the Netherlands, describes this basic principle, by contrasting it with the conventional logistics process. Variations on this logistics strategy are possible. For example, the INFILL KIT can be organized in separate packages, each delivered to the SHELL space in sequence on a JIT (just-in-time) basis. Or, some parts may be sent directly from the manufacturer to the SHELL for JIT installation. Good organization is key.

Comparing Logistics Strategies:

Traditional vs. Fit-Out

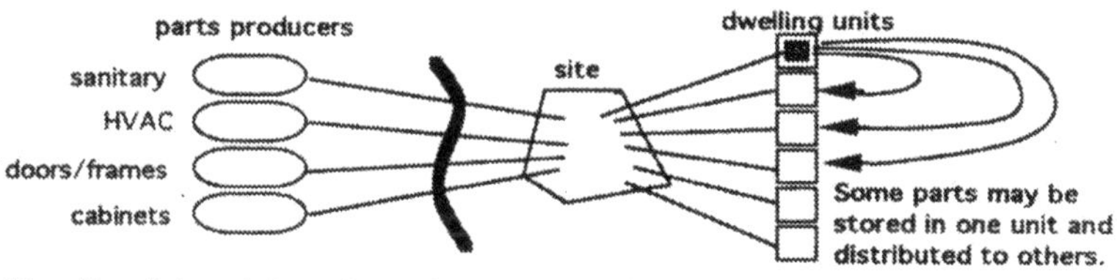

The Traditional Supply and Logistics Chain

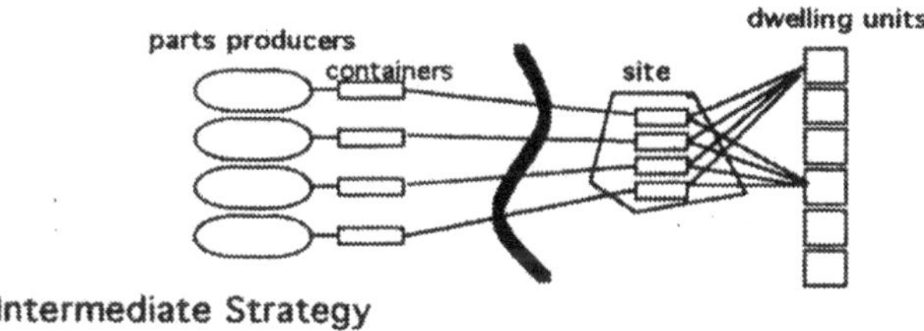

Intermediate Strategy

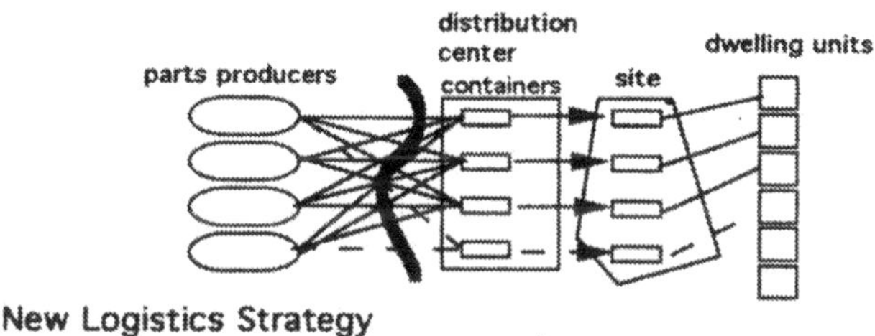

New Logistics Strategy

(source: Matura Netherlands BV)

Figure 8: Traditional vs New Logistics

Quality control through multi-skilled work teams

HOMEWORKS® uses work cells for the production and installation of INFILL kits. A number of industries outside the residential construction sector have embraced this concept. Work cells consist of multi-skilled workers organized in teams tasked with the responsibility of completing a designated production objective. Something like this is used in manufactured housing plants. Flexibility and product differentiation are two of the most important advantages of the adoption of the work cell approach.

Unlike the conventional trade-based sequence of work performed by separate subcontractors, INFILL kits are installed in an integrated way by the work cell, each member of which is multi-skilled for the complete task. Some tasks such as tile setting may require specialists.

This eliminates the management costs and other overhead of separate subcontractors. It also enables greater efficiency in the work as well as cultivating something like the guild culture lost in the movement towards hyper specialization.

Opportunities for mass-customization and product innovation

Housing construction is plagued by fragmentation and quality control problems, and has yet to fully embrace the new market dynamics of consumer-driven processes and flexible production. By organizing the preparation of INFILL kits in a controlled environment, using the most advanced information management software, fabrication technology and logistics, mass-customization techniques and processes help the construction sector meet customers' individual wishes and also meet stringent cost and scheduling requirements.

Using the idea of "virtual kits" (digitally displayed alternatives), marketing INFILL kits through the internet, reducing logistics complexity, and using interactive decision-making as a marketing tool, HOMEWORKS® points the way to a new way of combining efficiency and customization.

Long-term stock adaptability

The residential building stock now in place will need to last for many years, but it will face more changes than were expected when the stock was constructed.

Buildings that are designed for a specific demographic group or market niche face a more uncertain future than buildings designed with more generalized concepts of occupancy.

To meet the challenge of shifting demographics, life-styles and new technology, a new housing stock must therefore be inherently adaptable. Some argue that the conventional light frame building methods are inherently adaptable, with the cavities between floor joists and wall studs available for the distribution – and rearrangement - of pipes, wires and ducts. While this is true up to a point, the increased number, disorganization and entanglement of pipes, wires and ducts has made that presumption a myth in practice.

The SHELL – INFILL approach makes a calculated distinction regarding variable life cycle durability and utility of the parts making up a house. The most elegant approach would be to totally eliminate the practice of embedding pipes, wires and ducts inside the walls and floors that are likely to remain undisturbed for a very long time, and to hide them in a "layer" more akin to "thick paint" or "garments".

HOMEWORKS® initially makes a more modest proposal, embedding some piping and wiring in the SHELL while putting the rest in INFILL walls. This is described in Chapter 3. Other, more advanced solutions are available and can be introduced when the basic reorganization of the construction process is accepted.

General "FIXED-VARIABLE" Principle

This general principle, called "FIXED and VARIABLE", applies to design decisions at all design levels, as Figure 9 shows.

Figure 9: General Fixed-Variable Principle

Relation of SHELL Facades to INFILL

To the greatest extent possible, the building's exterior fenestration should be unlinked from the decisions concerning interior layout. However, some window openings may need to have variable window units installed as part of the INFILL decision when, for example a kitchen or bathroom is placed against a façade and the window sill is too low. (Figures 10, 11 and 12)

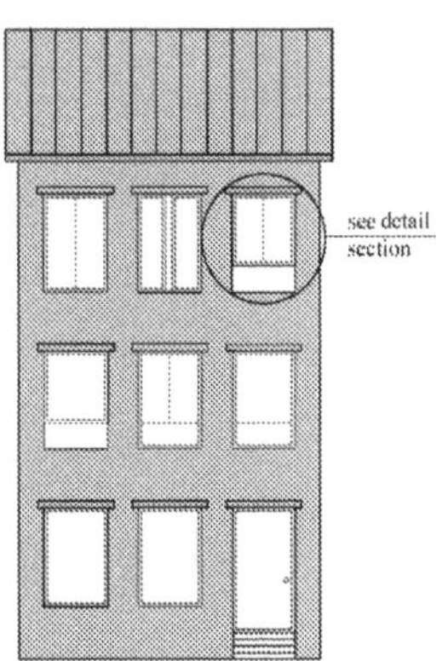

Figure 10: SHELL facade

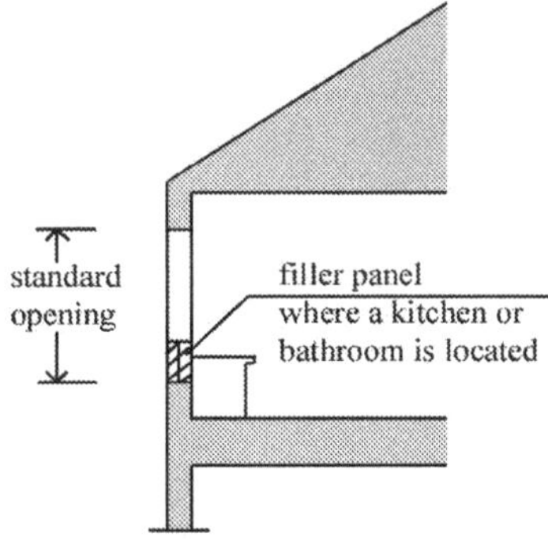

Figure 11: SHELL filter panel

Figure 12: An example of this principle in a house

Placement of SHELL window openings should be decided in part based on an analysis of likely infill wall placement options. For example, with a fixed window arrangement, interior wall "position zones" e.g. (A, B, C) can be defined, each with several wall placement possibilities. This allows a large range of layout variations in a given SHELL design. (Figures 13 and14)

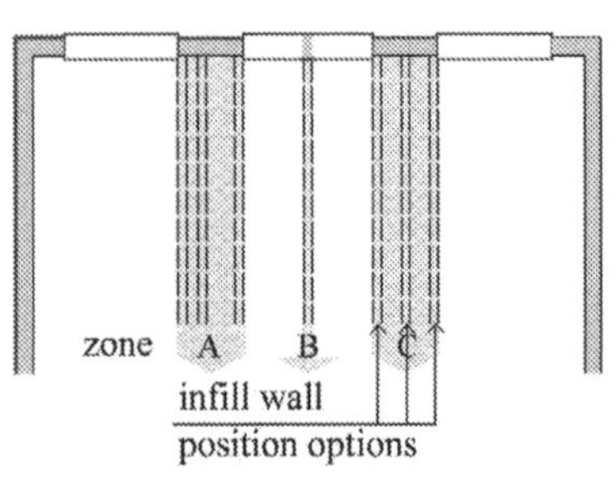

Figure 13: INFILL wall zones

a.
b.
c.
small room
middle room
large room
basic position opportunities
for infill partitions
1/2
1/2
a.
2/3
1/3
b.
1
c.

Figure 14: Room sizes vis-a-vis SHELL windows and dividers

General Interior Principles

To the greatest extent possible, once decisions are made on the location of kitchens, it should be possible to design different layouts or configurations of cabinets and equipment. (Figure15) The same should be possible with bathrooms.

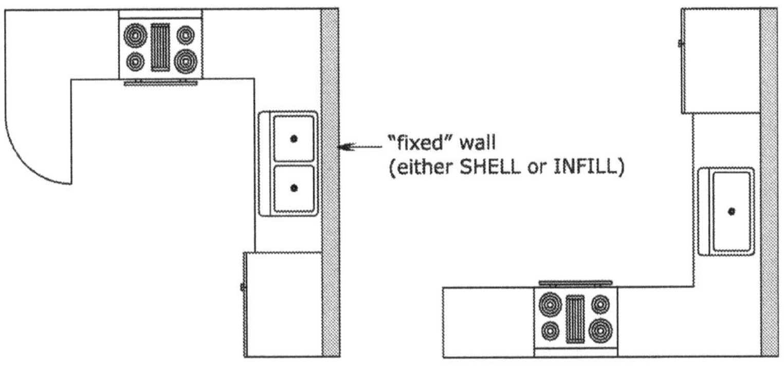

Figure 15: Kitchen layout variants

To the greatest extent possible, the interior surfaces of all SHELL walls and ceilings should have drywall installed as part of the SHELL contract. INFILL walls as part of a HOMEWORKS® kit attach to SHELL walls or floors using conventional mechanical connectors. (Figure 16)

SHELL floors are walk-able, using standard sub-floor materials or gyp-crete, if required, on wood framed floors, or a concrete slab on grade. (Figure 17)

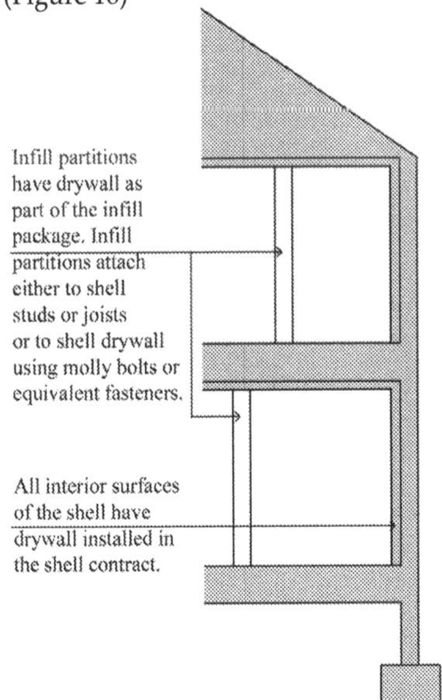

Figure 16: Walls

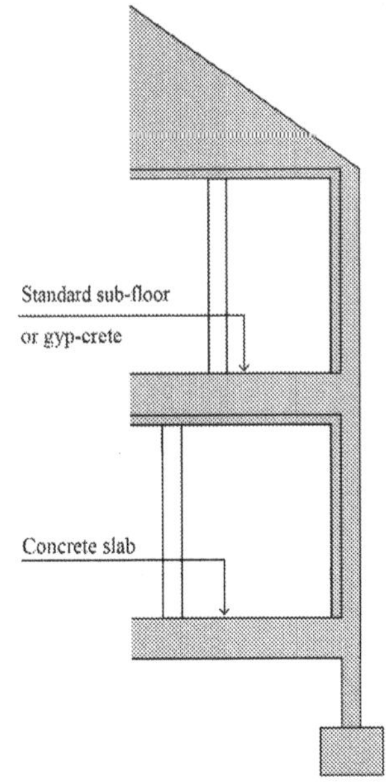

Figure 17: Floors

General Mechanical, Electrical, and Planning Principles

SHELL MEP systems are generally clustered in one or two vertical shafts. (Figure 18) Some SHELL MEP parts can be distributed within SHELL floors and walls, shown in Figures 20-26.

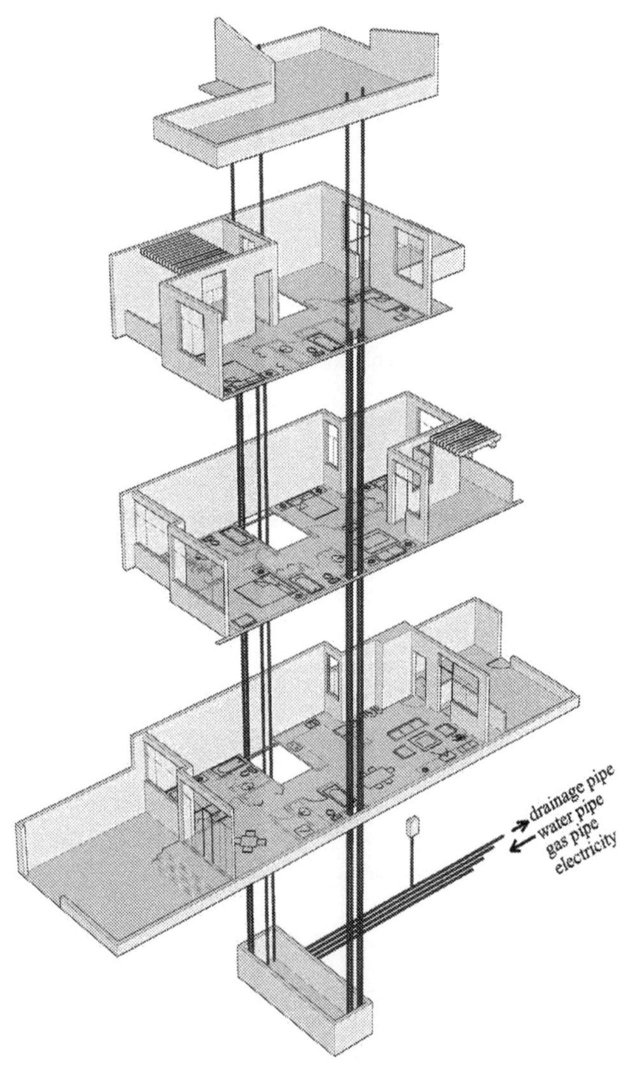

Figure 18: SHELL MEP stacks

To the greatest extent possible, the MEP systems (mechanical, electrical and plumbing) of one townhouse or dwelling unit should not pass through any adjacent dwelling unit. Utility connections from the public easement should go directly to each townhouse and not cross into the space of another townhouse. (Figure 19)

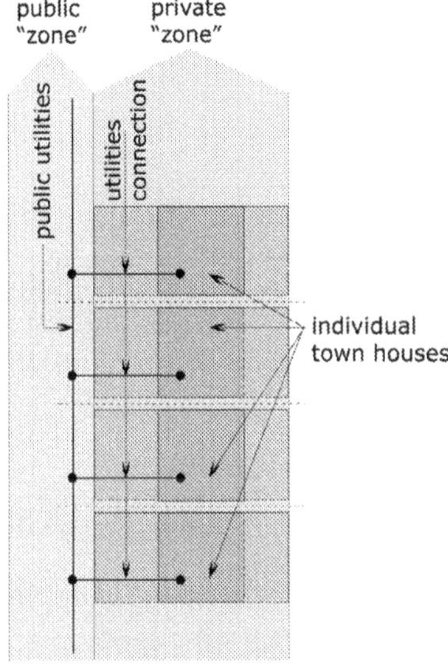

Figure 19: Independent utilities

To the greatest extent possible, decisions concerning the layout of rooms and their associated MEP systems on one floor of a multi-story townhouse should be independent of the layout decisions on other floors. This is important to the homebuyer's range of choices in the initial INFILL and subsequently. (Figure 20)

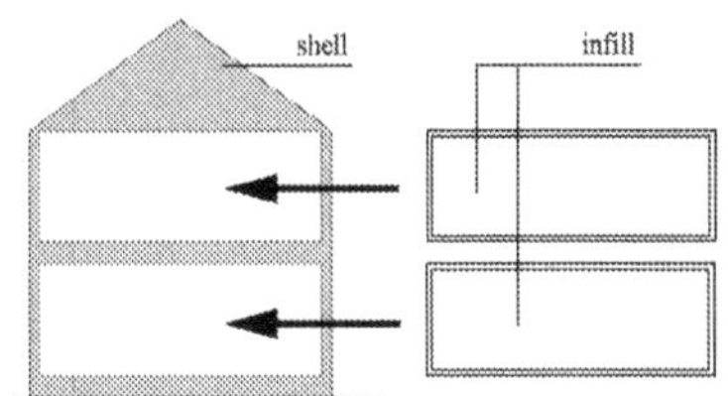

Figure 20: Independent layouts

Drainage

One of the most difficult utility systems to manage is drainage. To achieve the principles noted above, two basic positioning strategies are shown in the accompanying diagrams: The "above the floor" strategy will leave less floor space (because of the need for thicker walls) than the "in the trench w/ cover" strategy. In both cases, air-admittance valves are assumed instead of separate vent stacks. (Figures 21, 22 and 23)

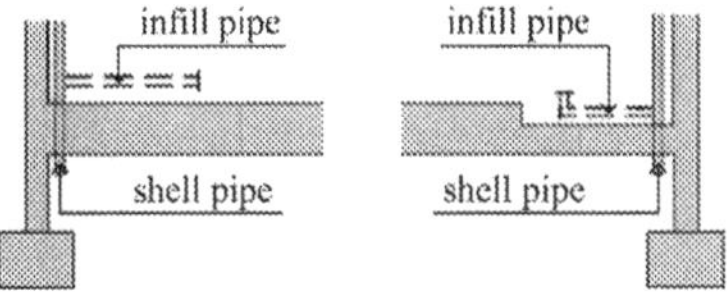

Figure 21: "Above-floor" on the left and "In-the-trench" on the right

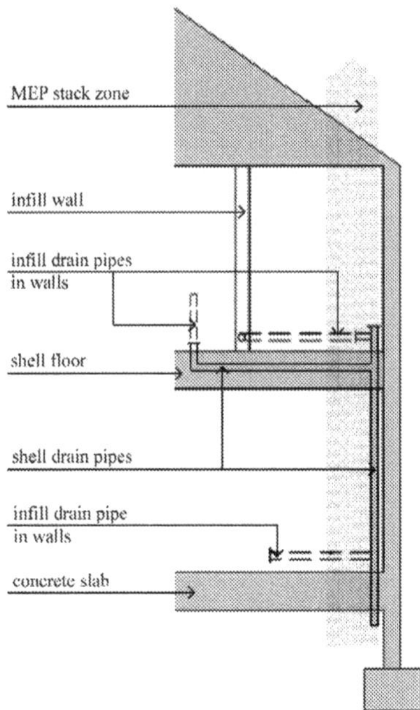

Figure 22: "Above-floor" strategy

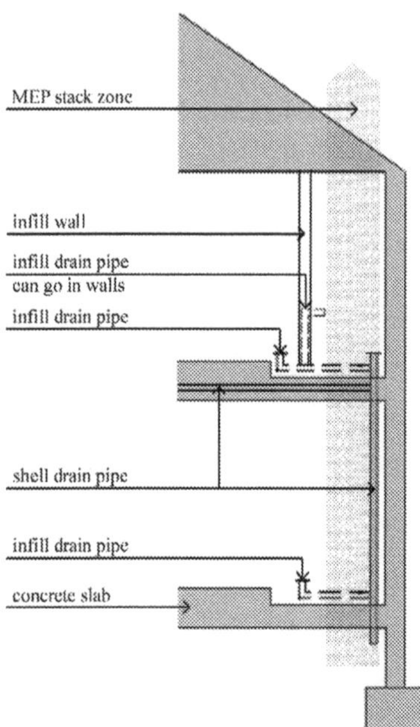

Figure 23: "In-the-trench" strategy

In the "above the floor" approach, horizontal drainage piping is organized in "drain piping zones" in certain "INFILL" walls, the lower zone accommodating the drain lines from toilets (floor mounted rear discharge fixtures), showers and bathtubs. The upper drainage zone accommodates drainage lines from sinks, washing machines and dishwashers. (Figure 24)

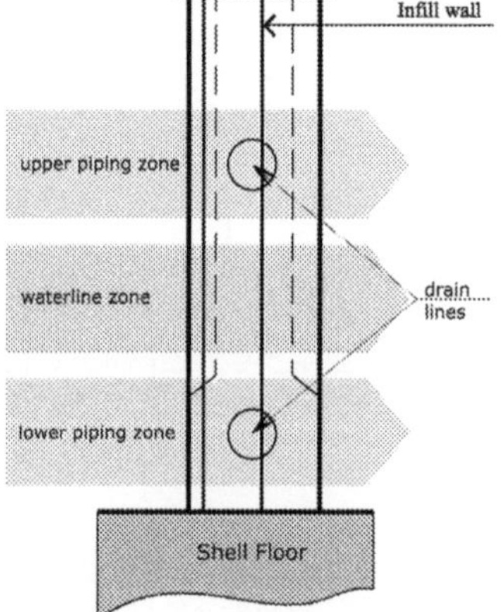

Figure 24: Horizontal piping zone

In some cases, horizontal drain lines can be placed behind cabinets. (Figure 25) In other cases, secondary INFILL walls are needed (partial or full height). (Figure 26)

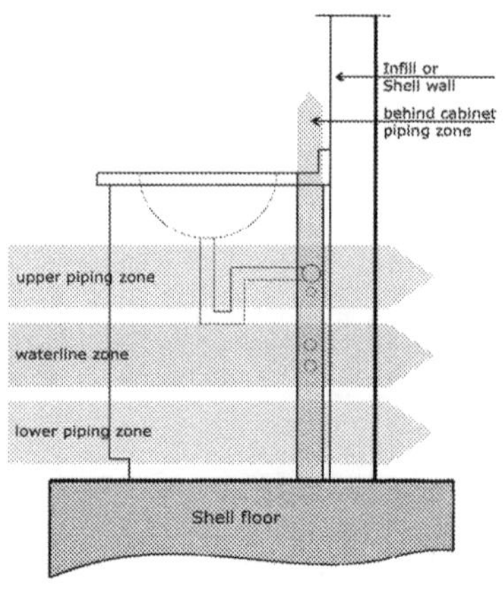

Figure 25: Behind cabinet zone

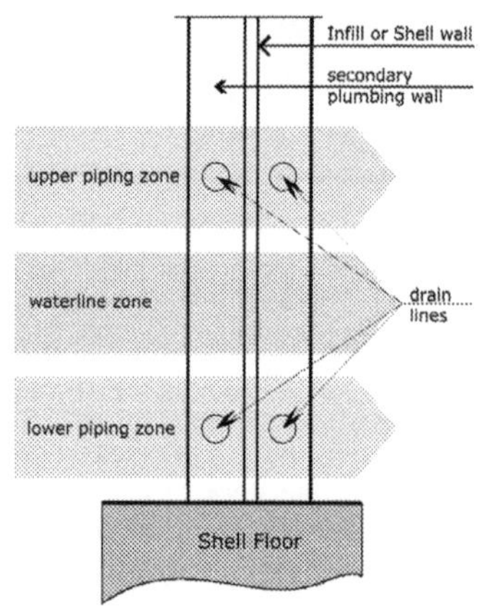

Figure 26: Secondary plumbing wall

Water Supply

The main SHELL water supply lines are located in the vertical shafts, as part of the SHELL design and construction contract. A distribution manifold is placed in the SHELL stack from which INFILL water supply lines are routed, either above the floor or in trenches covered as part of INFILL. (Figures 27 and 28)

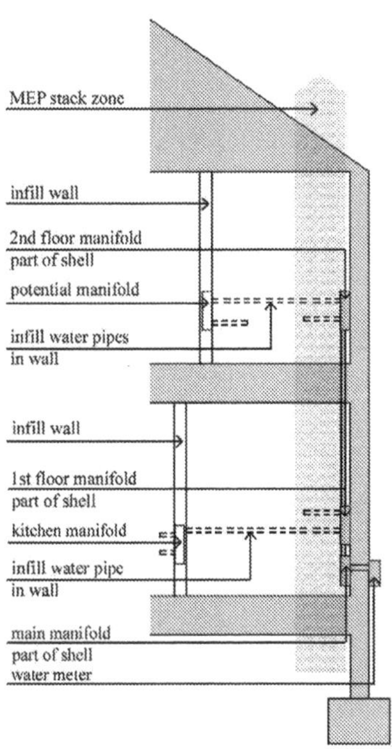

Figure 27: Above floor water piping

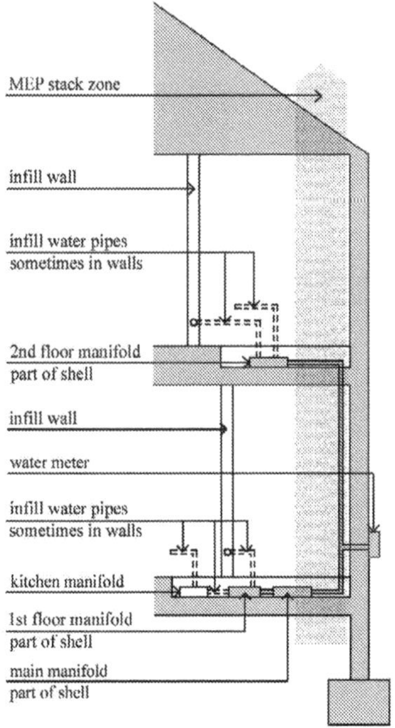

Figure 28: In-trench water piping

The horizontal water supply distribution that is part of the INFILL kit is further organized according to a hierarchy of distribution manifolds. This reduces the number of pipes at any given place in the INFILL. Horizontal water supply lines are distributed inside of INFILL partitions or behind cabinets. When horizontal water lines are in INFILL partitions, they must be placed in a "middle" zone between the drainage pipe zones (see diagram 24-25).

Water heaters can be centrally located or distributed closer to points of use.

HVAC (Heating, ventilation and air conditioning)

Since heat gain and loss of a given SHELL will be constant for any INFILL layout, most of the ductwork of a forced air system are located as part of the SHELL. The HVAC unit can be part of the SHELL or INFILL. The horizontal ducts can be embedded in the SHELL floors, with diffusers placed under windows at the SHELL's perimeter. This does not inhibit choice in location of INFILL partitions. (Figure 29)

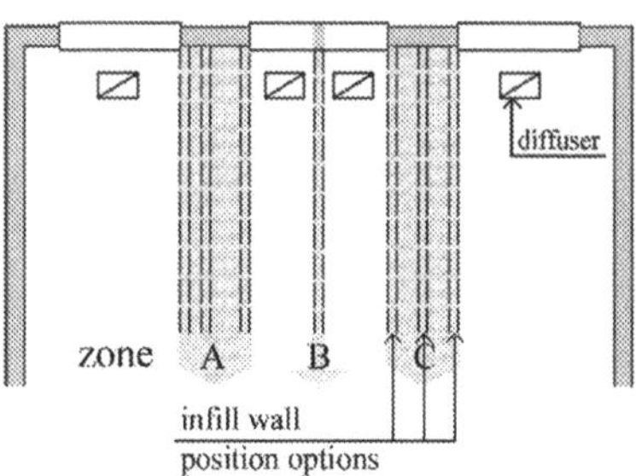

Figure 29: HVAC diffusers in SHELL

Main HVAC risers for supply and return, and exhaust for a gas boiler, as well as vertical ducts for bathroom and kitchen ventilation go in the main SHELL stacks.

Electrical and Data cabling

The SHELL will have at least two circuit breaker boxes after the meter base entry, for example one on each floor. Use of such sub-panels reduces the amount of cabling needed in either the SHELL or the INFILL kit. (Figure 30)

For example, the kitchen can be served by one main power line, with a distribution system as part of the cabinets. This dramatically reduces cabling from the main breaker panel and allows better integration of cabling and cabinets. (Figure 31 and 32) (examples from Holec in Europe)

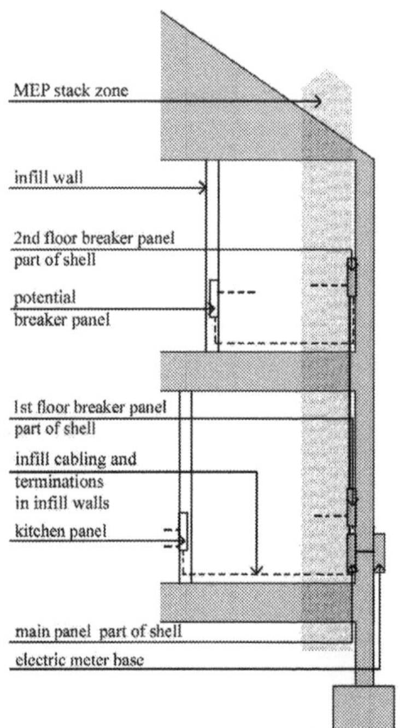

Figure 30: Sub-panel concept

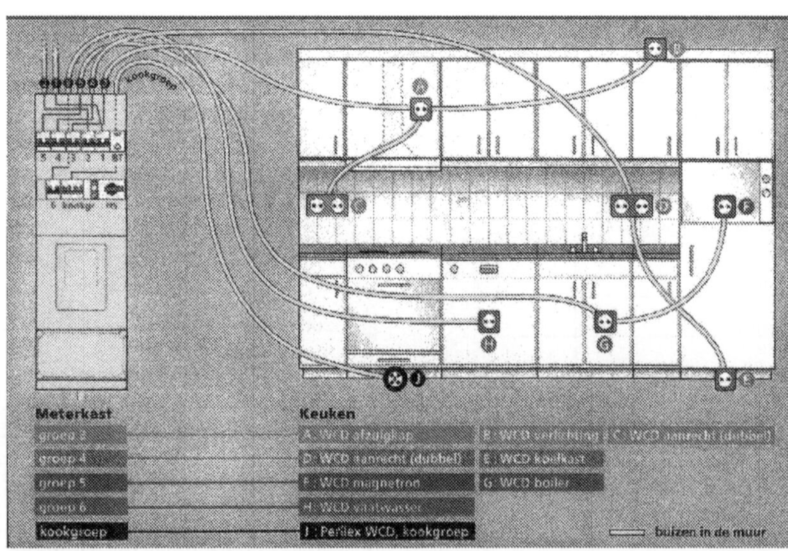

Figure 31: Traditional cabling to the kitchen

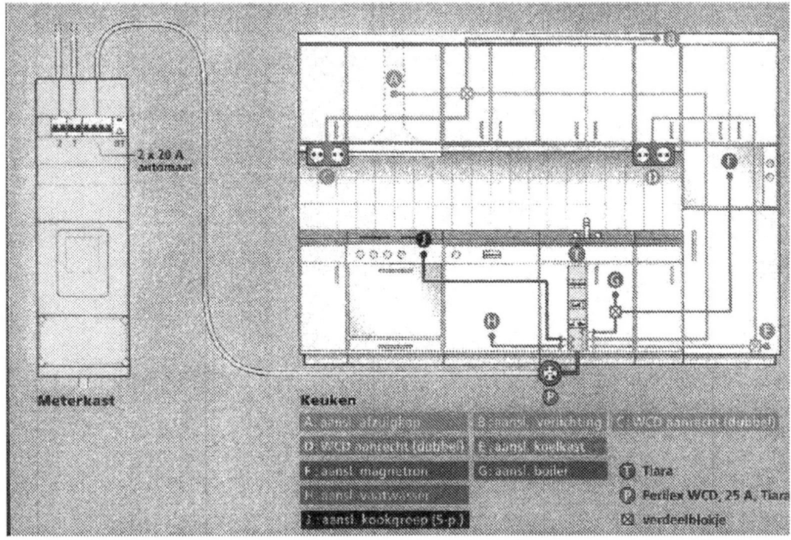

Figure 32: Integrated cabinet and cabling concept

Horizontal distribution of electrical and data cabling uses the Wiremold "Two-Piece Multiple Channel Non-Metallic Surface Raceway (Access 5000 Raceway). Since this system does not provide a suitable cable route under doorways, HOMEWORKS® provides a new technique requiring the invention of a new part to route cables under doorways and at points where lower zone drain lines interrupt the baseboard raceway. (Figures 33, 34, 35, 36, 37 and 38)

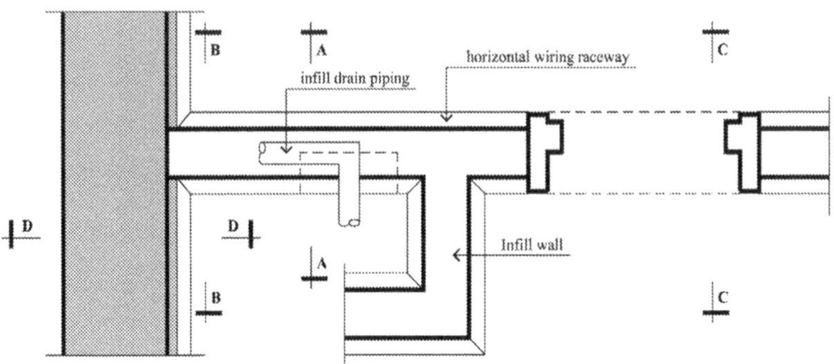

Figure 33: Key plan of HOMEWORKS® cable routing concept in INFILL walls

Figure 33 is a partial floor plan showing how HOMEWORKS® routes the main horizontal cabling (power and data). It shows part of the SHELL and an INFILL partition and a doorway. The sections indicated (AA, BB, CC and DD) are illustrated in more detail in the following diagrams. The main point of the diagrams is to illustrate the basic principle of channeling cabling in under-door thresholds, and where horizontal drainage pipes enter or leave INFILL partitions, in raceways within a sub-floor layer. This sub-floor can be a layer of one-inch thick homostote sheets or equal, and also serves as an acoustical barrier and leveler in preparation for the finish floor material.

Section AA shows the condition on an INFILL partition where a horizontal drain line in the "lower" zone serving a toilet interrupts a surface mounted horizontal wiring raceway. In some instances this interference may be avoided by omitting a wiring raceway in this position. But when both continuous cabling AND a horizontal drain line are needed as in Figure 34, a sub-floor wiring raceway is needed. (see also Figure 38)

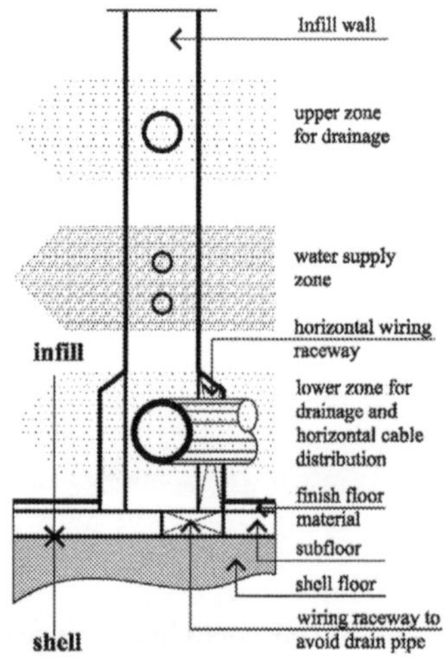

Figure 34: Section AA

Section BB in Figure 35 shows the condition in which a horizontal wiring raceway is needed on both sides of an INFILL wall.

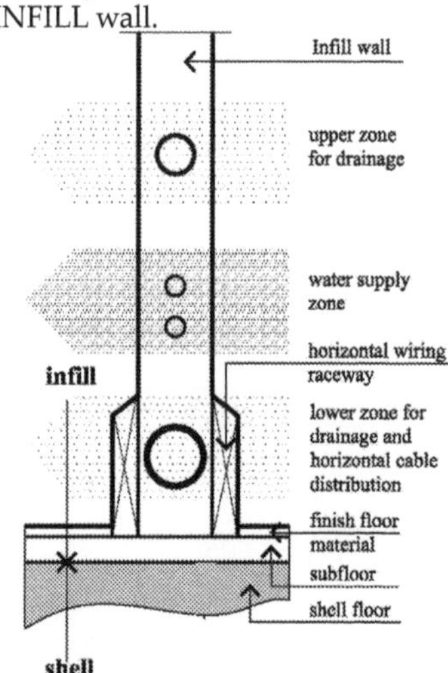

Figure 35: Section BB

Section CC in Figure 36 shows dual sub-floor wiring raceways at the door threshold. Each is dedicated to channeling cables (both power and data) from its corresponding horizontal wiring raceway on one side of the INFILL partition (see Figure 38 for more information on the new device needed to divert cable into the sub-floor raceway).

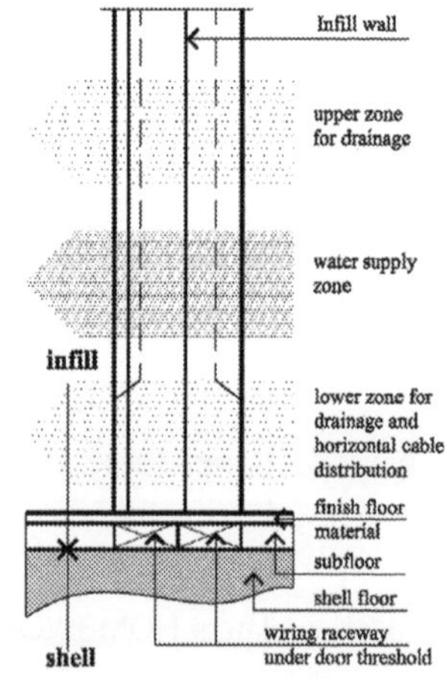

Figure 36: Section CC

Section DD in Figure 37 shows the horizontal wiring raceway at a SHELL wall. One principle reason for using a surface raceway is to avoid violating the thermal integrity of the SHELL. If, however, a vertical switch leg or outlet is needed in a SHELL wall, one of two approaches can be taken: a) penetrate the SHELL wall cavity and run the wiring there or b) add an additional "thin" INFILL wall whose cavities can be used for vertical wiring.

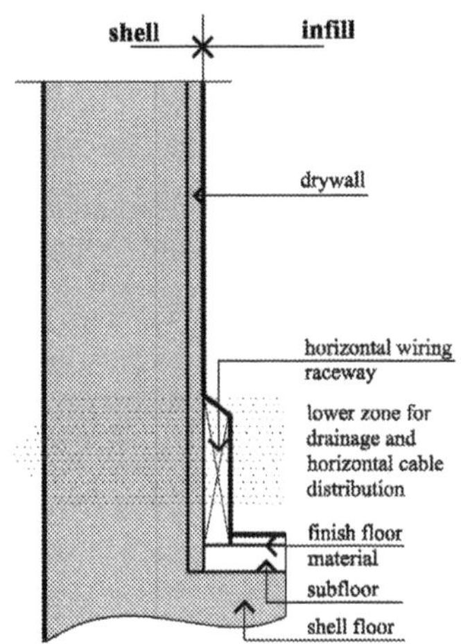

Figure 37: Section DD

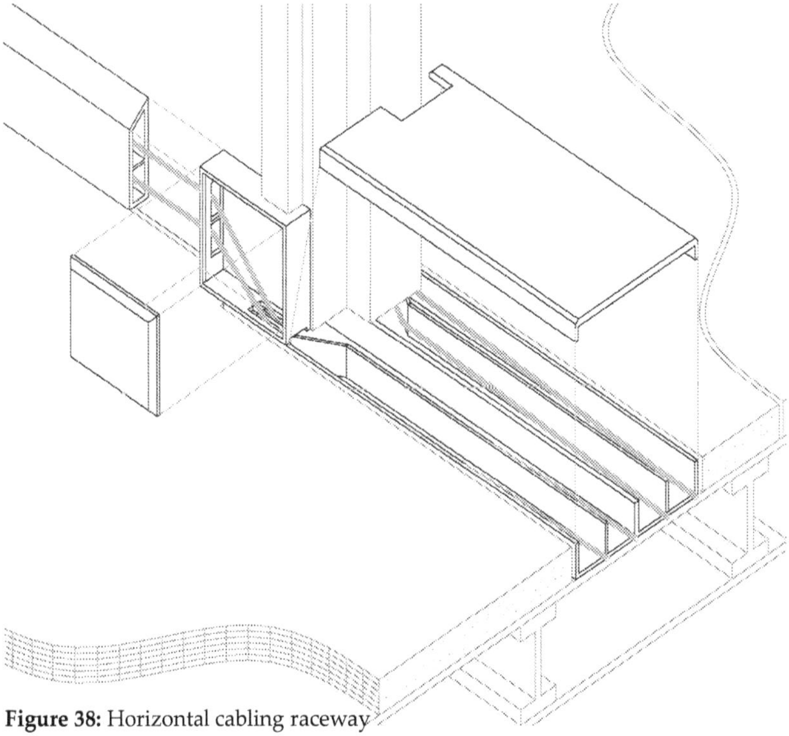

Figure 38: Horizontal cabling raceway

Figure 38 shows two key devices needed for a fully functional HOMEWORKS® wiring infrastructure. One is the cabling diverter box. This diverter's cover is coordinated with the selected doorframe and trim package. The other device is a vertical wiring mast, leading cables from the horizontal wiring raceway to a wall termination or wall lighting fixture. Where wireless controls are available, the use of such conduits may be reduced.

Ordinary products

One of the basic assumptions of HOMEWORKS® is that ordinarily available products are used to the greatest possible extent. The only exception suggested here is a cabling diverter needed to complete the power and low voltage cable distribution under doorways – as part of the INFILL kit. All other products needed to build a SHELL and to complete the installation of HOMEWORKS® are available in the market. In this sense, HOMEWORKS® is an "open system".

Some new processes required

To implement HOMEWORKS®; developers must be willing to build empty SHELLS, and either developers and / or homeowners must be willing to make INFILL decisions. The only way developers and homeowners will be willing to do this is that they are assured that one or more reputable INFILL companies exist to provide INFILL installation services.

HOMEWORKS® requires the use of work cells, as noted above. Without this, the approach will not succeed. This means that the earliest adoption of HOMEWORKS® may be in a merit shop labor environment where training of multi-skilled installation teams is possible.

As noted, the idea of kitting or product bundling goes hand in hand with skill bundling. In respect to product bundling or kitting, precedents exist. Electrical contractors "kit" electrical cables, boxes, and other parts in off-site shops to speed installation on-site and to assure quality. IKEA, the Swedish home furnishing company, provides "kits" to be assembled by the buyer. "Infill" is a kind of "IKEA + product bundle".

Existing CAD and data software can be modified

Existing CAD and information management software should be suited for HOMEWORKS® with some modifications.

Digittal fabrication processes may also be effective for the production of some parts of an Infill kit.

New business formation

No business equivalent to HOMEWORKS® exists for the residential market in the U.S. Other companies (e.g. OfficeRedi delivers just-in-time office interiors for such clients as H.R. Block, State Farm, and even kindergarten chains) operate in the same mode – fitting out "white box" spaces with everything needed for the operation of the company or organization occupying the space. Steelcase and other "office systems" companies offer products that do essentially the same thing for large corporate business clients, and other service providers exist operating in a similar mode, for branch banks, fast food restaurants, and so on.

A new start-up business is needed to bring HOMEWORKS to market. It should be located within 300 miles of several major urban markets. It should have good supplier relations with providers of the parts needed to make INFILL kits.

HOMEWORKS® is targeted for both the urban and suburban townhouse market as well as for the urban elevator building type – either new construction or adaptive reuse / conversion market. We have made other detailed studies suggesting the efficacy of this approach in conversion of obsolete office buildings to residential use.

Task Partitioning

House building is ordinarily subject to task partitioning to get the work done. Exactly how to partition the work can be an issue. Technical and organizational issues are involved, including distribution of responsibility and initiative.

A few notes on this matter are in order, on the basis of which the specific task partitioning embodied in HOMEWORKS® will make more sense.

Partitioning Based on the Distinction of Designing and Building

One division in house production is between designing and building. One party proposes what should be made, and another party makes it. Communication is needed between these parties, and usually a "design" is the vehicle for that communication – some sort of representation of what is agreed should be made.

Partitioning Based on Specializations

Once this partitioning is made, many additional partitions can be found, inside the domain of designing and also in the domain of making. Specialists are evident in each domain, providing detailed representations or work, following partitioning based on accepted specializations. In the domain of designing, we have architects, engineers, interior designers, and so on. In the domain of making, we have project managers, carpenters, electricians, plumbers, and so on.

Partitioning Based on the Distinction of Project-specific and Project-independent Parts

Another kind of partitioning found in house building is the production (design and making) of both "project-specific" and "project-independent" parts. The former kind of parts are "pulled" into being by the project – whether made on the spot of use or made elsewhere and brought to the site of use (these are called prefabricated parts). The latter (project-independent parts) are "pushed" into being by the initiative of the producer and thus made available to any project for use. The latter constitutes the world of manufactured parts.

Increasingly, manufacturers are learning to harness the tools of production developed to "push" products into the market for the production of parts "pulled" into being by a user. This is called "mass-customization".

Partitioning Based on Order of Installation

Another way of partitioning in house building is based on the order of installation. While variations exist, the usual order of building is driven by gravity (foundations precede floors, and walls follow the floors they sit on, etc). Another conventional order of installation is that the harder or stiffer parts go in first, followed by the more malleable or bendable parts. Thus the plumber usually precedes the electrician.

Partitioning Based on Estimated Life Span Value and Control Patterns

Another basis for task partitioning has its roots in differential durability of use of parts. Parts (physical systems and spaces) deemed suitable for a specific estimated life span value are organized as a 'whole". This is conventional practice in the office market where base buildings are constructed with an expected life, to be filled in by tenant work with shorter expected life span value. A similar practice is used in the construction of large shopping centers.

Scope of Work

Each of the possible ways of partitioning work noted above has its own issues of defining and specifying the scope of work in each task. In general, the longer the practice of partitioning has been conventional, the easier it is for all parties involved to do their work unencumbered by complex negotiations and problems of information exchange.

Disputes over jurisdictions of responsibility nevertheless arise when new products are introduced (which specialty trade gets control?) or when practices change.

The dispute between architects and interior designers still lingers and remains a source of conflict. Trade jurisdiction disputes between craft unions still occur, although as the labor unions loose power in the construction sector, these conflicts are of less significance than before.

In the early days of the now conventional practice in office buildings and shopping center development, when the distinction of base building and fit-out was first coming into currency, scope of work definitions were more problematic than today.

In practice today, everyone is more relaxed about the problem of scope definition and while legal advice is normally sought, the procedures and habits are well understood.

But where this particular task partitioning pattern is new, conflict is almost inevitable, particularly when control of the "parts" is distributed to different service providers.

Careful study of the issue of task partitioning and definition of scope of work is needed to make HOMEWORKS work.

Without a good understanding of these problems, a new business attempting to bring HOMEWORKS to market will stumble badly.

Technical Interfaces

Technical interfaces exist on three levels. At each level, interfaces are normally identified according to their spatial position, their physical dimensions and material properties. Generally, interfaces are predicated on the principle that the part with the longest expected use value will be installed first, in such a way that parts with shorter expected use value attached to them can be removed with little or no degradation of the part installed earlier.

Many thousands of technical interfaces exist in a HOMEWORKS® townhouse, as in any house. Some interfaces of a HOMEWORKS® house are identical to those in any conventional townhouse, but some are new in one respect or another.

To avoid problems, these interfaces need to be identified and specified, preferably on a performance basis, leaving decision-makers a number of alternative solutions and materials. This decision-making flexibility should extend beyond the initial design and installation to include provisions for future alterations.

The Regulatory Environment for HOMEWORKS®

The public regulatory environment for townhouse construction should protect the legitimate public interest in public health and safety. While doing so, the regulatory environment should also set the conditions for maximum autonomy of the sphere of action, represented in HOMEWORKS® by the INFILL kit.

Today, in large part because of the extreme entanglement of the "public" and "private" portions of houses (particularly the MEP systems), this distinction is virtually impossible to make in practice. In addition, a massive amount of residential renovation and repair work is undertaken outside public regulatory approval, because no one wants to bother with what is perceived as a burdensome regulatory process. Further, the home project centers sell everything needed to do the work without distinction as to whether the buyer will submit to building inspection or not. This can cause technical problems with implications on public safety and welfare as well as on insurance claims, in large part because the two spheres of action are not clearly distinguished.

In the most basic reformulation of this regulatory distinction between "public" and "private", all decisions that implicate other houses should be subject to local regulatory oversight, based on national model codes. This includes the foundations, main utility connections, the building structure and façade. It should also include provisions for effective energy conservation embodied in the SHELL and performance requirements for the heating and air conditioning system and fixtures using public utilities such as water and sewage.

On the other hand, national product and systems approval bodies such as the Underwriters Laboratory should have jurisdiction over all decisions that are made within the "private" sphere of responsibility, concerning the selection and placement of products with no consequence to other houses. These decisions should be liberated as much as possible from the burden of local regulatory approvals, and conversely local building officials should be freed from unnecessary responsibilities so they can do better work in the sphere that makes sense for them as public servants.

Today, decisions in the "private" sphere include the entire spectrum of consumer electronics, appliances and communications devices. It would be unthinkable that a local inspector would need to approve plugging in a new computer or microwave oven, or the addition of a new wall or door, or the installation of new kitchen cabinets.

HOMEWORKS® essentially pushes the boundary between the "public" and "individual" sphere "upstream" and, by careful planning and safe technology, brings more decision-making into the "private" sphere, unencumbered by what happens "next door".

Process rigidity and inability to respond to market "pull"

Where uniformity of product is acceptable, a "Model T" approach to the design and delivery of houses makes sense. In this model of production, the problem is to optimize the whole and engineer its efficient delivery, managing supply chains, approvals and marketing accordingly. As the essay at the end of this monograph points out, the resulting process rigidity was the "Achilles Heel" of the early "industrialized housing" efforts. This was the idea of "pushing" products into the market. It is also the main drawback of most conventional housing production today.

The problem is that this industrial model, once the most powerful organizational concept for manufacturing, is no longer useful except for the lowest "commodity" products for which competition is weak or nonexistent, or for which there is a public monopoly. When competition is strong and the market is "pulling", the unitary industrial model fails to deliver requisite variety.

Building production has never been entirely congruent with the "Model T" approach. The reason is that a building is not a product in the same way that an automobile or a refrigerator is. A building is a one-of-a-kind thing that exists in a specific place and is approved by local political processes. Of course a building is made of many manufactured products each of which is the result of initiatives by producers to push products into the market.

Increasingly each of these products is understood as a "consumer product"; this is changing the behavior and the organizational strategy of the companies producing these products. Windows are a good example. Now, large catalogues are available from which to choose, and some degree of customization beyond the catalogue is also offered. This portends an important shift away from the old "Model T" scheme, but the shift has not yet reached the production of houses per se.

Technical and organizational entanglement

While manufacturers of specific building parts like windows or kitchens are moving toward a more consumer-oriented "mass-cuatomization" mode of production, contractors or developers of whole houses have not yet been able to make that same transition. The key reason is the excessive technical and organizational entanglement of the whole house process.

One of the primary – and inevitable - organizational entanglements that binds the construction of buildings (as opposed to cars or windows) is the public/private boundary that buildings straddle. On the one hand, houses (even the most remote, but certainly urban houses) exist in the public realm – regulated and taxed by public bodies, attached to a public transportation infrastructure, and utterly dependent on public utilities and services. In this sense, houses conform to an idea of a "common good".

On the other hand, houses are private property, are bought and sold in the real estate market, and are financed by private lenders. In this sense, houses are personal possessions and are one of the most valued ways to express individuality in our society – witness the emphasis on home-ownership as opposed to rented apartments.

The tension arising from complex interdependencies between these two forces brings increasing conflict today in the field of building construction. This is caused by building methods and organizational forms that do not allow a sufficiently clear distinction between them. Lacking that distinction, freedom to innovate is inhibited in both spheres.

Obstruction of innovation and manufacturing "push"

Because of the excessive interdependency between the two spheres of action mentioned above, innovation in both spheres is less robust and progressive than, for example, in the transportation sector. There, because the road and the vehicle are autonomous but related by rules and regulations developed in public-private processes, we see steady incremental development in highway technology on the one hand and vehicle technology on the other. This analogy should not be taken too far. But it makes the point that when buildings can be conceived more clearly as standing with one foot in the field of public oversight and the other in the field of the consumer market, we may see the flowering of more innovation in both spheres than is otherwise possible. The key is to sharpen the distinction between these two spheres of action, while at the same time refining and coordinating interfaces between them. (see Chapter 6)

Excessive waste in materials and labor

Houses change over time. The statistics on remodeling show that more money is now spent on remodeling and repairing houses than on the total investment in new construction. This will only increase, for many reasons.

But the amount of waste generated by remodeling and repairing is also massive and excessive, and shows no signs of slowing down. Landfills in urban areas are overflowing and refuse is trucked to neighboring states at high cost. Not only is this process ultimately unsustainable from an environmental perspective, it is not sensible economically.

Houses should be more durable, but this performance requirement is seemingly at odds with the prevalence of remodeling. It is rare that a discussion of durability is couched in terms that recognize the forces of change. The correct formulation of durability in houses should be durability of the whole because the parts can change, albeit at varying cycles.

A correct conceptualization of the whole house into parts according to life cycle value and the public/ private distinction may make sense in solving the problem of excessive waste in construction and remodeling.

The second area in which conventional construction is wasteful is in the deployment of labor. It is well known that skilled labor is increasingly hard to find. Secondly, development organizations are faced with a problem of sequencing various trades on dispersed projects. A project manager spends each day driving from house to house finding the right labor crew to go to a specific house to complete a task, then has to instruct them which house to go to next. The inefficiency is obvious and the management cost is excessive while adding little value to the final result.

Conclusion

This report has been written primarily for North American audiences. However, certain basic principles may well apply in other "building cultures". While intended for North American builders, housing producers, architects and real estate developers, it is written from the perspective of international developments toward "open building".

The separation of a base building from the interior fit-out has become normal for office buildings and shopping centers. All parties now unquestioningly follow this practice - building regulators, financing institutions, designers, construction companies, product manufacturers and certainly developers.

This approach is now finding application in hospital construction, principally as a way to control complexity and change.

Around the world, this approach is beginning to be applied – for purely commercial reasons - in residential architecture with notable success in Japan, the Netherlands, Russia and Finland. Both developers and homeowners are gravitating to this approach because they find it to be to their advantage. The most advanced cases now use advanced software to manage the information flows and coordination and in Finland, recent projects use the internet as a tool to support user choice.

In the United States, some developers intuitively seem to understand the distinction presented here, especially in the conversion of old office buildings to housing. But few if any have formalized the approach to take maximum advantage. The only exception seems to be Bensonwood Homes, a Timber Frame company.

HOMEWORKS® is based on the author's detailed knowledge of the technical and managerial aspects of this way of working. It should thus be seen as a reference to professional designers, builders, manufacturers and developers.

The result of long time research and experimentation, this report comes at a time when housing practitioners in all disciplines in the United States are looking for better ways - ways to make residential construction more responsive to individual user demand, more efficient in its execution and more sustainable over time.

It is now time for commercial interests in the US to take the initiative by adopting the approach presented here. By doing so, there is good reason to think that the result will be improvement in the process of delivering wood frame or "2x4" housing. The benefits should be felt in the lives of homeowners, and in the quality of the experience of those building our houses.

Appendices

1 Untangling the American House

2 Where to get more information

3 Notes on Attribution and Sources

Appendix 1 Untangling the American House

A visit to an ordinary dwelling or apartment building under construction in any neighborhood in the United States, just before the sheetrock is hung, is a good way to assess the state of entanglement in American house-building.

Imagine what we will see (Fig.1). Amidst the normal jumble of building-in-progress, the smell of sawdust, remnants of wiring insulation, dried mud and debris on the sub-floor, and empty styro-foam hamburger containers, a keen observer will see the exposed wall and ceiling cavities jammed full of parts. Immediately evident is an almost unbelievably confused array of installed pipes of varying types and sizes for supplying and carrying away fluids, air ducts of several shapes for moving air, thousands of feet of wires for electric power and communications, and, in some jurisdictions and some building types, sprinkler lines for fire suppression.

Fig.1 The entangled service systems in the floor cavity of a normal residential project, 1993.

It was only five generations ago, around the time my grandfather was in his teens, that plumbing and central heating, and later wiring, became commercially available at reasonable costs and were promoted by architects, developers and manufacturers for use in apartment buildings and houses.[1] These entrails now dominate housing processes in ways unimagined at that time or even thirty years ago.

A State of Entanglement

In virtually all construction types, multi-family and detached, wood frame and concrete, the technical and organizational entanglement of American residential building has reached a critical state. The overall disorder in the relation between the pipes, wires and ducts, and the rest of the buildings they serve, is an indication of the problem.

Fig.2 A balloon frame house in 1935. (*The Architectural Record,* August 1935.)

This largely random interweaving of parts lacks the clarity and elegance still attributed to wood framing or other structural systems per se. Today, walls and floors of sticks of wood or substitute materials — the main elements of the beloved and ordinary 2x4 system that first came into use in the 1830s in Chicago[2] (Fig.2) - are filled to overflowing. The wooden or light-guage steel structural elements are fastened in place. Then, pipes, wires, and ducts are knitted haphazardly into them. This is especially destructive now in traditional wood-frame construction, where holes are bored and chopped out on-site as needed - often at random by each trade - and often with no coordination.

Each part of these service and structural systems no doubt represents, in itself, the best product for the least cost, available from the world-wide building products industry, each installed by a different trade and each serving a perceived need.

This interweaving process seems to have worked up to now for four main reasons: the remarkable structural redundancy and forgiveness of wood or steel framing; the expectation that the next stage of work in this conventional chain of events will cover any depredations of the previous player; the relatively low cost of materials; and the availability of sufficiently low-wage but skilled workers. None of these can be taken for granted today.

Because the cavities between wall studs in all construction types and floor joists in framed buildings have been available by nature of frame construction, they have been filled, in no particular anticipatory order, in a historical progression by the first to get there. Trade jurisdiction work rules, starting in the craft guilds but now dominating the work force in general, followed the emergence of new parts and processes, dividing the work accordingly. Now, separation of work by trade is as antiquated and problematic as the paradigm of house building they accompany and may well be its Achilles heel.

The entanglement portrayed here is the fault of no one in particular. This fact makes it difficult to assign cause or to assess responsibility. It is therefore difficult to remedy. In an important way, the diffused responsibility so characteristic of this "system" is both its liability and its strength: it is a living system controlled by no one trade or company but is shared and gradually improved by all who use it.[3]

The Interplay of Technical and Organizational Patterns

The situation of entanglement would not be such a problem if it were only technical in nature. However, as with many situations made visible by observing the behavior of technical hardware, the issues are not divorced from their organizational and social ambiance.

Now, the entire constellation of actors - manufacturers, designers, constructors, regulators, and house occupants - is likewise enmeshed, producing conditions ripe for poor quality, higher costs, legal disputes, and loss of decision flexibility. Not only that, this kind of entanglement thwarts innovation, because innovation occurs best when the interdependency among systems parts is low.

Among the many social and organizational forces at work, five stand out.

Demographic Churn

Most of us have read about or directly experienced the shifting demographics in our neighborhoods and regions, including changes of household types and sizes. For example, in many urban neighborhoods, over a twenty or thirty year period, the sociological structure may change, in terms of income and household structure. Two basic things will happen in that case; occupants who want to stay in the neighborhood will modify the dwelling stock, or families will move out if such changes are infeasible or too expensive.

If the building stock does not become obsolete in a short time, it at least may not make a good fit with the next statistical cohort of households. While in a very large aggregate sense all of these mismatches may sort themselves out, in any one building or locale the discontinuity can have telling but difficult to measure negative effects on household well-being, contributing to a sense of powerlessness over the place of dwelling at a very personal level. Because dwellings mean the most to us as inhabitants, such effects are often felt in the community at large.[4]

Decision Deferment

We also know that, in larger housing developments that take several years from planning to occupancy, developers face a dilemma. On the one hand they will seek to defer the costliest decisions and most-likely-to-change decisions as long as possible. They want to keep their options open at all levels – from number of units to color of cabinets and fixtures. But the impulse to delay sends ripples through the entire chain of actors, pushing all action to the last possible moment, compressing an already difficult and entangled process. Unless well organized, this decision-deferment process can cause major cost and construction management conflicts. The only other choice for a builder is to simply fix all decisions and ignore pressures for decision flexibility.

Control

Many households want a direct say in major interior layout, fixtures, and equipment decisions, no longer content with moving into dwellings someone else has decided have good layouts and feel. This may be a case of households wanting to reclaim control of housing decisions from remote experts, experts who, often lacking other means, base decisions on statistics rather than actual individuals. Organizing for variety without driving up costs is a constant challenge for builders and development teams. Many are pushing variety as far as they can within the present production paradigm.[5]

Change

Industry statistics show clearly that expenditures on house renovations, adaptations, and upgrading are now well beyond $100 billion each year in the U.S. market.[6] These commitments to dwelling adaptation are more difficult and expensive for both professionals and do-it-yourselfers to realize because of the entanglements of parts and the parties involved, as discussions with contractors or building owners and inhabitants reveal.

Organizational and Supply Chain Reconfigurations

Finally, many industries are reorganizing their supply chains in response to new concepts of value creation. Ikea is an example of a large organization, with sophisticated supply constellations, that offers a new division of labor, including customers who assume certain key tasks of assembling well designed but lower-cost products. Home project chains such as Lowes and Home Depot represent other organizations restructuring to new demands. These companies offer surprisingly comprehensive design and construction services and the logistics to make it happen. The concept of "mass customization" is now discussed among industry forecasters, including the Global Business Network in California. Robert Reich, Secretary of the Department of Labor, discusses the concept of "multi-disciplinary work cells" in a recent book.[7] The United Brotherhood of Carpenters and Joiners now takes interest in new cross-trade affiliations to alleviate jurisdictional disputes, and was recently exploring various proactive training and apprenticeship programs that they believe might be needed in the future, as unions seek market recovery in residential construction against the merit shop contractors.[8]

The latter reconfigurations, taking place nationally and internationally, are good examples of responses to new social, economic, and technical conditions having a direct bearing on housing processes.

An important complexity threshold seems to have been crossed, in a fascinating incremental process accomplished without anyone noticing. We have come to a point in which the autonomy to act individually is being drastically reduced. The opportunity is being lost to change a decision or adapt what is already built, without engaging - often in conflict - dozens of other actors, each controlling some physical parts, each with their own problems and priorities.

This is truly a situation of loss of freedom across the board, not at all what we have expected from our way of building houses and the mythic democratic, market-driven house building culture that has grown up with it. This loss is remarkable because it is happening in a political economy that we have traditionally associated in ideological terms with individual autonomy and control in housing processes.

Paradoxically, in a society stressing individual rights and responsibilities, we find that decisions by occupants, apart from expensive custom-designed single- family houses, are considered a nuisance by housing experts who dominate the housing market at all points in its supply channels. This view, which still holds a constricted view of efficiency and is based on obsolete concepts of standardization and unified expert control, is very much at odds with the kind of healthy housing activities we now need.

A Short History of Entanglement

Early American Houses

American houses built in the eighteenth and nineteenth centuries are a good background against which to trace the evolution of our present entanglement, because then, neither electricity, plumbing, nor central heating had entered the houses of their time (Fig.3).

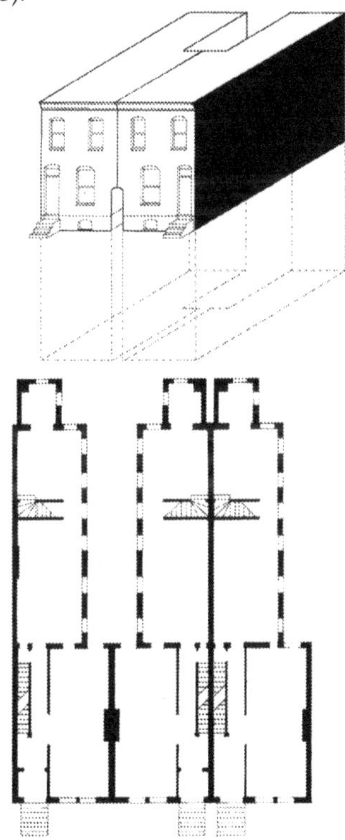

Fig. 3 Plans of nineteenth century row houses in Reading, Pa., showing kitchen and bathroom as appendages at the rear. (Steven Holl, *Rural & Urban house Types in North America*, pamphlet Architecture 9, New York, 1982.)

In these early houses, often following principles of compositional clarity and formal simplicity brought from European traditions[9], the few spaces were organized in such a way that they could be and were used for many household activities. Often, sleeping, living, bathing, and cooking occurred in one space in a time-sharing approach. It was normal to have change of use in harmony with the seasons and, of course, rearrangements of furniture and light partitions and storage elements such as wardrobes, armoires, and the like when a new family moved into a house.

Rooms were labeled "hall," "north parlor," "south parlor," "chamber," etc. Few could afford to build use-specific rooms. Indoor toilets and bathrooms were nonexistent, and kitchens were found in any room where a fireplace provided a place to cook or were located in a shed attached to the back of the house.

Houses of the Industrial Revolution

During the last half of the nineteenth century, indoor plumbing for water distribution and drainage was gradually and then rapidly introduced into houses and apartments, accompanying rapid urbanization, gradual increase in household affluence, and justified fears of threats to public health, safety, and welfare. This was supported by the development of inexpensive, mass-produced, cast-iron and lead piping, and public water systems. The first vented trap to remove sewer gases from toilet rooms was introduced in 1875, the introduction of the first really sanitary water closets took place about 1890, and publicly funded sewers and waste treatment plants were built in the same era. These public and private initiatives enabled bathrooms to migrate, in stages, from the privies in backyards to attached toilet rooms tacked onto the back of houses, and finally to take their place inside, even in multifamily apartment buildings.[10] (Fig.4) Building regulations in most large cities required indoor plumbing by the end of the nineteenth century.[11] Even so, 45 percent of households did not have complete indoor plumbing as late as 1940.[12]

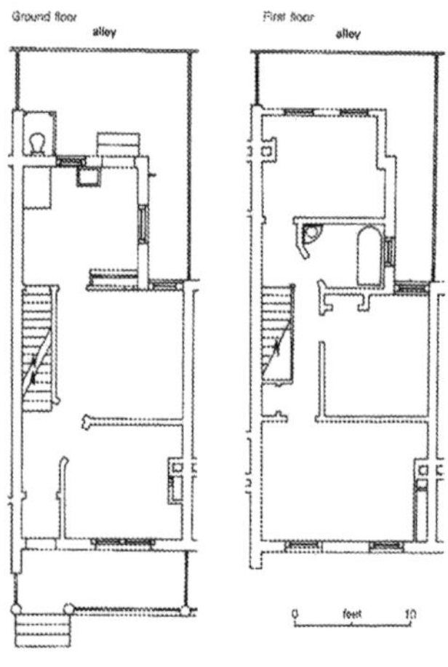

Fig.4 A plan of a Philadelphia mechanic's house in the early twentieth century, showing a kitchen in the rearmost space, a toilet attached to the back of the house, and a bathroom without toilet on the second floor. (Parish, H.L., *One Million People in Small Houses,* Philadelphia, 1911.)

Other pipes brought natural gas to give illumination (a short-lived technology), and still other pipes brought steam for heat. In the period between 1900 and 1920, wires began twining through walls and floors and behind baseboards, replacing gas as a means of illumination and serving a burgeoning supply of electrical appliances plugged into convenience outlets.[13]

The mechanical removal of odors and humidity, and the addition of cooling to the technical services, with additional equipment and distribution lines and ductwork, waited until decades later to make an appearance inside houses as standard features. Then, these developments happened quickly, in the span of several generations, following World War II.

Functionalism

The migration indoors of bathrooms and kitchens attached to their resource tethers, taking place from the 1880s onward, coincided with the Victorian concept of dividing indoor space into distinct "functional" territories.[14] Particularly with the detached house, the concept of a spatial order related to specific uses was a distinct departure from long traditions. These traditions were rooted, in many cases, in the relative autonomy of "spatial type" and "function". In many instances of the same type, "functions" and "territorial distributions" would be decided by those who inhabited the same type.[15]

Thus, during the Industrial Revolution, house design experienced an important evolution. From spatial and geometric orders offering a certain capacity for a variety of habitation patterns, house design took on functional determinism. This way of thinking locked in specific uses by two means: the arrangement of walls tightly wrapped around the spatial requirements of an activity, and the attachment of resource tethers serving these specialized spaces. In short, spatial arrangements and uses, distributed for reasons established by convention even prior to the introduction of mechanical systems, were now captives both of "arrangement and dimension based on function" and the resource systems needed to serve them. Thus, cooking equipment went into spaces previously called "kitchen" prior to gas and electric appliances, and bedrooms became special purpose spaces by the introduction of built-in closets, replacing wardrobes and movable cabinets, which had previously allowed any space to be a sleeping room.

There were efforts, however, to radically re-think the distribution of services in houses in ways independent of the particular distribution of functions or uses in a house. In 1869, for instance, Catharine Beecher's proposal for an American Woman's House clustered all services in a central core serving all rooms in the house, each claiming adjacency to the central core.[16] (Fig.5)

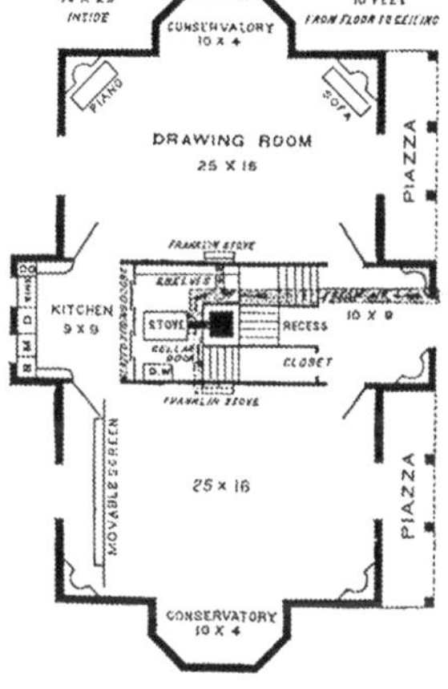

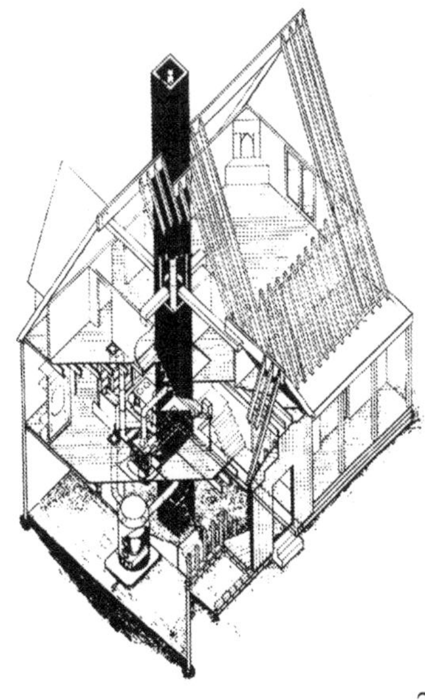

Fig.5 Drawing of the central utility core proposed by Catharine Beecher in 1869. (from *The American Woman's Home,* Catharine E. Beecher and Harriet Beecher Stowe, 1869, in Russell, Barry, *Building Systems, Industrialization and Architecture,* Wiley, New York, 1981.)

Much later, but in the same spirit of efficiency and rational planning, Richard Buckminster Fuller's first Dymaxion House of 1927 had a central mechanical and structural core from which services were to be distributed to surrounding living spaces. He made this proposal while criticizing what he called the International Bauhaus Movement's superficial approach to mechanical systems, an approach that, he said, "never went back of the wall-surface to look at the plumbing...." This was an important but seldom voiced criticism of a movement that had been precipitated in the early 20th century by the invasion of houses and streets by mechanical services.[17] The criticism was accurate, but the proposal seems to have missed the mark, given what is known today. (Fig.6)

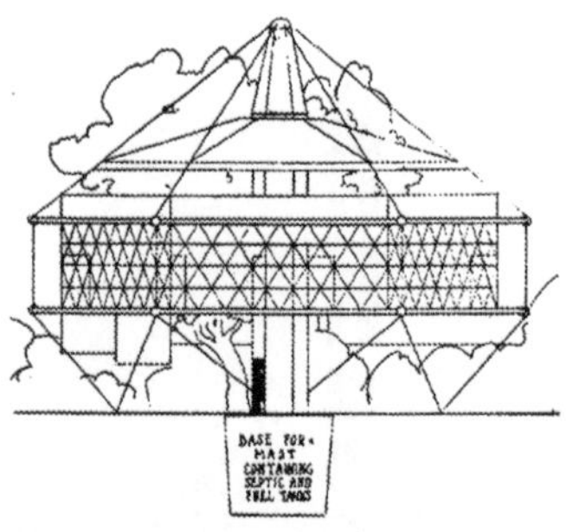

Fig.6 R. Buckmiunster Fuller's Dymaxion house, showing a central service core. (*Building Systems, Industrialization and Architecture,* Wiley, New York, 1981.)

These early efforts at promoting a "standardized, functional" mechanical core for all houses can still be seen in standardized floor plans in so-called "low cost housing schemes" in which bathrooms and kitchens are repetitively back-to-back, an arrangement argued to be more efficient and less costly than dispersed utility spaces. While this efficiency argument may have held at one time in circumstances of bureaucratic management, it has certainly not been particularly relevant as a "standard" in the American experience, except when organizations based on bureaucratic control have built for an economic class assumed to be permanent and denied control of the act of dwelling. Even here, doubts are beginning to surface about the correctness of those assumptions, given the realities of housing dynamics.

Early Years of Experimentation

The building technology and architectural journals of the 1930s, following directly on the new and widespread availability of resource distribution systems in houses, document tremendous experimentation with improvements in house building technology. This surge of inventiveness, almost all of which sprang from private initiative, lasted until the Second World War and took place during the Great Depression when relatively few new buildings were built. Aside from the experimental work focused on new construction, much of the practical effort of the time focused on correcting and modernizing existing buildings with new mechanical systems, efforts that accelerated after the Housing Act of 1937 and the formation of the Housing and Home Financing Agency in the same period. (Fig.7)

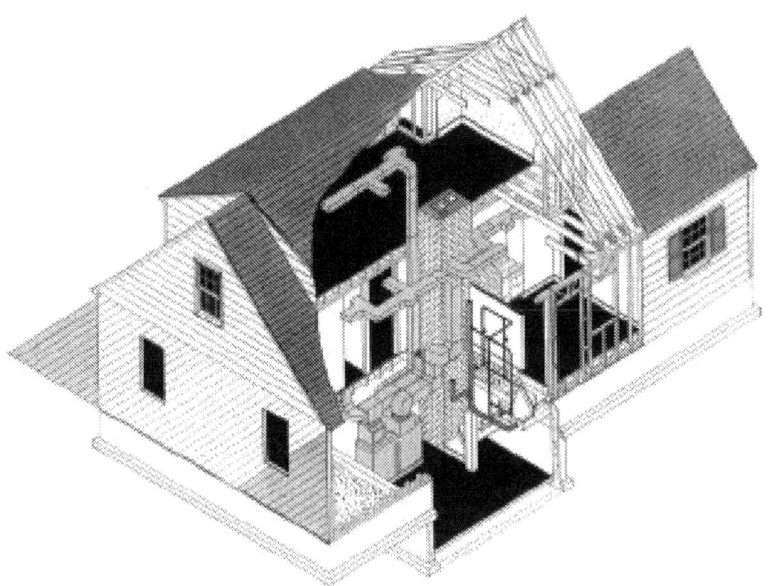

Fig.7 An integrated house from the Modern Housing of Washington, D.C., development. —"In its construction, modular design, standardized plans, a studied production "flow pattern," and novel construction practices combine to effect substantial cost-and time-savings..." (*The Architectural Forum,* November 1937)

Despite or perhaps because of the newly introduced resource systems, these experimental efforts from the 1930s reveal a curious lack of attention to these systems. With only a few exceptions, published accounts in the architectural press of the time focused on new ideas for the space-defining elements of houses, their construction, and appearance: walls, floors, roofs, foundations, and all the elements of which they are made. At the same time, most ignored or only grudgingly accommodated the pipes, ducts, and wires needed to make the houses livable.

In these schemes, if cavity walls of new materials and shapes were proposed - and many were - the new resource systems must have been assumed to go between, inside, and through the cavities, but often this information is not available. Some explicitly stated that this was the intention. When solid-core prefabricated walls and floors were proposed - and there were and still are many - there is seldom any mention of where wiring, piping, and duct work are to be placed. Presumably, they are placed in dropped ceiling plenums, hidden in closets, or otherwise "put in afterwards."

The reason these systems – at that time still relatively new - largely escaped the attention of the architectural and building inventions of the 1930s is worthy of speculation in more depth than can be accomplished here. But whatever paradigm was at work then is still at work today: these non-architectural elements will be put in later, after the important work - usually, in architectural thought, the structure and spatial enclosure - is completed, or more mysteriously, they will be "integrated."

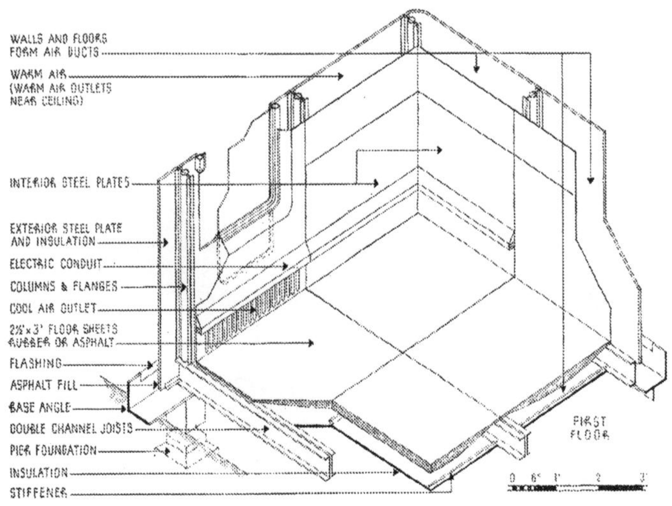

Fig.8 A diagram of a Van Ness Steel House. *(The Architectural Record, 1935.)*

Many fine histories of housing design, technology, and production chronicle the period from World War II to the early 1970s when the Operation Breakthrough project of the federal government closed its books. After that, the literature becomes markedly thin, as though all the enthusiasm of the previous fifty years had dissipated.

A careful reading of efforts that were recorded reveals only passing references to the creeping entanglement involving pipes, ducts, and wires. This absence is understandable, since, until the widespread introduction of forced air for heating in the late 1940s and air conditioning in the late 1960s, the technical repertoire had not changed markedly for over forty years. (Fig.8, 9) For example, by the 1940 census, fewer than 58 percent of households had central heating.[18]

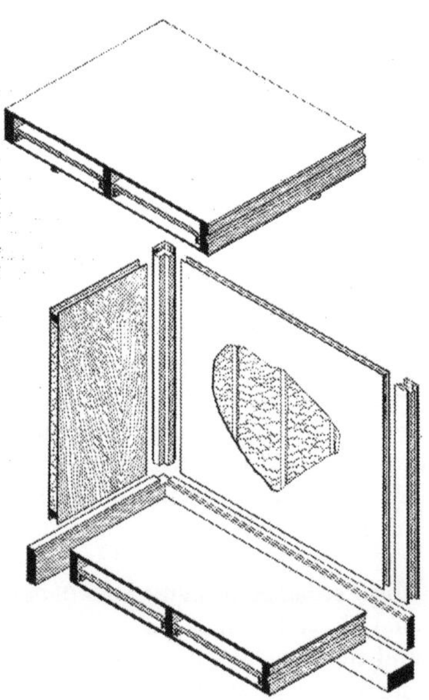

Fig.9 A prefabricated all-wood house assembly. *(The Architectural Record,* August 1935.)

Integration

When resource systems are mentioned at all in the housing innovation literature during the period after 1972, the discussions are frequently framed in terms of systems integration. This is a concept that has directly or indirectly dominated much of the research thinking about housing and other building technology since the 1960s.[19]

The basic principle of integration is to put as many subsystems as possible into one unified assembly. This was, and in some quarters still is, thought to be the key to better performance. This approach can be described as an effort to rationalize and standardize the physical positioning of discrete parts currently installed separately in buildings: pipes, wires, and ducts, within floors and walls. Many proposals have suggested that integrated assemblies could be standardized to enable their mass production. In what now seems a curious linkage, this strategy was thought to be a way to achieve "flexible" and "adaptable" housing schemes.[20]

Whereas placement of service lines within walls and floors could, on a project-by-project basis, meet the highly variable demands of construction and market requirements until recently, efforts to standardize this intricate interweaving - and thus reduce me variety of configurations - could not possibly succeed. No one wanted to build standard floor plans in large enough numbers to make an investment in such mass-produced, high value-added, integrated component production worthwhile.

This was especially so as increasingly complex systems were introduced in the last twenty years: more sophisticated and complex heating and cooling systems with humidification and dehumidification, central vacuum systems and other appliances and fixtures each requiring several service hook-ups, separated black and gray water drainage lines, home-run domestic water supply piping, more power and communications cabling, a diversification of power or energy sources, ventilation systems, fire suppression sprinkler systems, and the like.

By the late 1980s and into the 1990's, faith in systems integration had reached a high pitch, with renewed efforts at the US Department of Housing and Urban Development's PATH initiative (Partnership in Advancing Technology in Housing) developed in close partnership with the National Association of Homebuilders Research Center.

Systems complexity had increased, demand for variety had continued unabated, but no new paradigm had emerged on the scene of the American housing industry to help sort out and simplify the tasks. Little if no evidence was available that the goal of improving quality, durability, energy efficiency and flexibility would be accomplished with the paradigms in currency.

Shedding the Limitations of Functionalism and Entanglement

The principle direction of thinking dominating housing technology up to now, can be called the *unibody / integration* view. This view corresponds closely to attitudes held in currency by many industry leaders, writers, and academics into the early 21st century.

But this paradigm is now obsolete. It is fundamentally a static, technical view in the narrow sense, trapped in a model of centralized control and standardization. Because of this, it is unsympathetic to the full reality of healthy housing processes in the United States.

The *unibody / integration* perspective ignores one old reality and one new idea in housing, which the state of entanglement we have now reached compels us to recognize. We are now in a position to shed the limitations of functionalism and entanglement.

The first old reality – easily ignored in the deeply ingrained (but now questioned) cultural propensity to focus on "new" - is the fact that undergo gradual, fine-grained adaptation to remain current and healthy. This is a process often initiated by households or for their benefit, making for a widely distributed pattern of control. This is pervasive, constituting a vital economic and social activity, only partially accounted for.

The second idea is the use of levels. Levels concern the way the built environment organizes itself hierarchically according to the distribution of control over it.[21] This later concept is evident in nonresidential projects such as office buildings and retail facilities, where it has been conventional practice for some time in the U.S. to manage design, construction and management on the basis of levels. In these projects, a "base building" is constructed, consisting of load-bearing elements, public spaces, and common mechanical systems. This part of the whole is designed to have a long lifespan. Filling in the empty spaces - the "fit-out" – follows, with each occupant deciding individually what suits their requirements and budget. This process of "fitting-out" continues as long as the building stands.

The facts of change and distributed control converge in the levels concept. The base building is meant to be "fixed" relative to the more variable "fit-out". One party (the aggregate of individual occupants or a landlord) controls the base building. A number of independent parties each controls its "fit-out," retaining a degree of technical and legal autonomy and responsibility.

This approach is applied as a matter of course in the office and retail sector. It may have merit in U.S. housing as well, to liberate a process now so entangled. A model of this practice has been patiently moving forward in the Netherlands, Finland and Japan. Hundreds of housing units have been built using it. One product developed to aid this was the Matura Infill System. (Fig.10) According to people doing the work in these countries, new multifamily residential projects, as well as renovations in both the subsidized and private markets, are being built using the levels approach. In them, base buildings are being "fitted out" with units meeting household preferences, at a cost equal to the *unibody / integrated* approach, which is conventional there too and equally outmoded. These projects offer developers the new benefit of matching rather than anticipating user requirements and getting the work done more quickly than before. They demonstrate how variety, previously considered to be the source of higher cost and more difficulty, can actually be more efficient.[22]

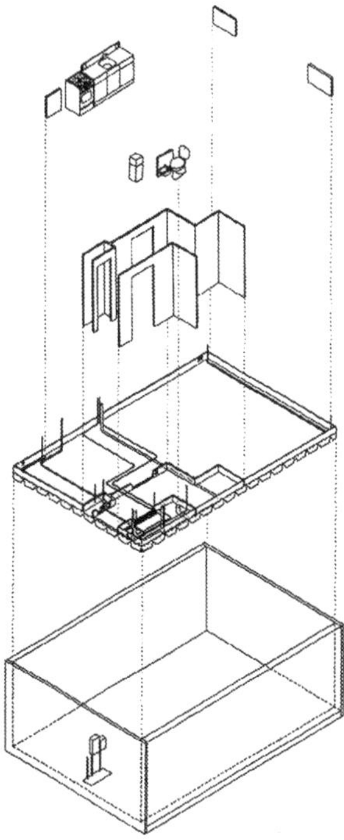

Fig. 10 A diagram of a dwelling organized on the principle of base building and fit-out. All installations specific to the dwelling are in the fit-out, except for the main supply and return pipes and ducts. This approach is applicable to both new construction and renovation. Matura Netherlands. (from *Entangled Building?* (ed) E. Vreedenburgh. OBOM, Technical University Delft, The Netherlands, 1992.)

This base building/fit-out approach also has an interesting dimension that should satisfy architectural formalists and functionalists alike. Well-designed base buildings can be constructed following sound and enduring architectural principles, offering capacity and giving opportunity for a wide variety of unit sizes and floor plan layouts. Thus, architects and builders can literally "give" form and space to others who then have the freedom to occupy the given forms in their own and changing ways. It is an important kind of organized hand-off in a complex process, one which may now be able to respect the fundamental need for historical continuity at the level of the building as part of the public environment, while respecting the need for continuous though slow cultivation of the interior spaces in respect to evolving household needs.

A Turning Point in Housing

A real turning point in meeting the problem of entanglement in American housing will come when several events occur. First, wiring, piping, and duct management following the unibody/integrated paradigm in currency today - "just put the pipes and ducts in the cavities or anywhere they will fit" - will have to become an economic burden to most actors in the housing game, especially builders and consumers. It may already have reached this point.

Second, there will have to be widespread recognition of the magnitude of investments in altering existing dwellings as a percentage of total investments in housing. This data is relatively well known, but our building traditions are only slowly waking up and adjusting to this reality.

Third, the unibody/integration model will have to be displaced by the levels model as a normal basis for organizing complexity and variety. Despite the many differences between commercial projects and housing - differences in their respective places in our social, economic, and cultural fabric - the base building/fit-out strategy is a useful model that should be carefully studied and tested in housing practice. This was recently recognized in the NSF-PATH sponsored National Housing Agenda Workshop.[23]

The reality of technical entanglement is being recognized in many industries and countries. It is given many different names, "sorting out, "design for assembly," "disentangling," "base building/fit-out," "working on levels." There are, however, advantages beyond those gained in solving technical problems, critical as they are to improving the state of the art in housing. The concepts of levels and the principle of disentanglement also enable us to rethink again the organizational question of the balance between the community and the individual, mediated as always through the control of the built environment.

A visit to a multifamily residential project under construction and organized this new way offers a tangible image. Opening the front door of the dwelling unit, our future occupant sees an enclosed but empty space, with columns or bearing walls at certain locations, and exposed vertical plumbing and ventilation lines in a cluster. With the assistance of a designer, or by referring to several prepared model-unit designs, an interior design is prepared matching our household's preferences perfectly. Because a sophisticated computer software program is used, the design is transmitted directly to an off-site facility where all specified parts - including parts for making walls, all equipment, cabinets, fixtures, piping and wiring, and heating and cooling equipment - are prepared or organized. One week after the order has been placed, this package of parts is transported to the building, or delivered in just-in-time bundles, accompanied by a trained, four-person installation crew. In a carefully choreographed sequence, parts are brought into the dwelling space and installed. After installation of the fit-out is complete, carpet installers arrive, followed by drapery hangers, and the furniture is brought in. The elapsed time between the initial visit to the bare space and completed fit-out and occupancy is less than three weeks for an average size dwelling, at a cost equal to that charged by a developer using the conventional approach, and offering the additional advantage that future changes will be easier to accomplish."

This scenario represents a new paradigm. The question is how to shift paradigms. We need to learn how to intentionally embark on a new concept pathway, on which each will find opportunities unavailable if the path isn't established in the first place.

References

1. Wright, Gwendolyn. Building the Dream, A Social History of Housing in America. Pantheon Books, New York, 1981.
2. Gideon, Sigfried. Space, Time and Architecture, The Growth of a New Tradition. Harvard University Press, Cambridge, 1963.
3. Habraken, N. John. Transformations of the Site. Awater Press, Cambridge, 1988.
4. Gallagher, Winifred. The Power of Place. Poseidon Press, 1993.
5. Author's personal interviews with major homebuilders.
6.. National Association of Homebuilders. The Future of Home Building; 1991-1993 and Beyond. Washington, D.C., 1991.
7. Reich, Robert, Tales of a New America, Random House, New York, 1988.
8. Author's personal conversations with Edward Gorman, Carpenter's Health and Safety Fund of North America, United Brotherhood of Carpenters and Joiners.
9. Holl, Steven. Rural and Urban

House Types in North America. Pamphlet Architecture 9, New York, 1982.
10. Nielsen, Louis S. Standard Plumb in Engineering Design. McGraw-Hill, New York, 1963.
11. Ventre, Francis E. "Building Regulation." Dictionary of Art, McMillan, New York (upcoming).
12. Two Hundred Years of U.S. Census Taking: Population and Housing Questions 1790-1990. Bureau of the Census, Washington, D.C., Nov.1989.
13. Nye, David E. Electrifying America, Social Meanings of a New Technology, 1880-1940. MIT Press, Cambridge, 1991.
14. Wright, Gwendolyn, op cit.
15. Habraken, N. John. Type as Social Agreement." Biannual Asian Congress of Architects, Seoul, 1988.
16. Russell, Barry. Building Systems, Industrialization, and Architecture. Wiley, New York, 1981.
17. Banham, Reyner. Theory and Design in the First Machine Age. Praeger, New York, 1960.
18. Two Hundred Years of U.S. Census Taking: Population and Housing Questions, 1790-1990. Bureau of the Census, Washington, D.C., Nov.1989.
19. Bender, Richard; Wilson, Forrest (ed). A Crack in the Rear View Mirror. Van Nostrand, New York, 1973.
20. Kendall, Stephen. "Flexible Design, Encyclopedia of Housing, Garland, New York (upcoming).
21. Habraken, N. John. "Culuvating the Built Field," Places. MIT Press, Cambridge (upcoming).
22. Kendall, Stephen. "Open Building for Housing. Progressive Architecture, Nov.1993.
23. NSF/PATH Housing Research Agenda Workshop. Volume I & II. Michigan State University, June 2004.

This paper was first published in BLUEPRINTS, the journal of the National Building Museum, Washington, DC, vol xii, no. 1, Winter 1994, under the title "The Entangled American House".

Websites

Building Futures Institute
Ball State University
www.bsu.edu/bfi

John Habraken's website
www.habraken.com

OBOM Strategic Studies
TU Delft
http://www.obom.org/

4-MET Center
Tokyo Metropolitan University
http://www.4-met.org/index-e.htm

Architecture Institute of Japan Open Building Sub Committee
http://news-sv.aij.or.jp/keikakusub/s13/

Bensonwood Homes
http://www.bensonwood.com/company/openbuilt.html

MIT Open Source Building Alliance
http://architecture.mit.edu/~kll/OSBA_proposal.htm

Open House International
http://www.openhouse-int.com/

Helsinki University of Technology, Department of Architecture
http://www.tkk.fi/Yksikot/Osastot/A/AR/eng/index.htm

CIB W104 - Open Building Implementation
http://open-building.org

Partial Bibliography of Sources on Residential Open Building

Fassbinder, Helga, Jos van Eldonk, *Flexible Fixation, the paradox of Dutch housing architecture* (Van Gorcum, Assen/Maastricht: Eindhoven University of Technology, 1990, 81p.).

Fassbinder, H. J. van Eldonk, "Flexibilität im Niederländischen Wohnungsbau". *Architecture Plus, 100/101* (1998, p. 65-73).

Habraken, N. J., *Three R's For Housing*, (Amsterdam: Scheltema and Holkema, 1970).

Habraken, N. J., etal., *Variations: The Systematic Design of Supports* (Laboratory of Architecture and Planning, MIT, Cambridge, 1976).

Habraken, N. J., *SUPPORTS: An Alternative to Mass Housing* (U.K.: Urban International Press, Second English edition, 1999).

Kendall, Stephen, "Who's in Charge of Housing Innovation? Vernacular construction technologies distribute control widely," *Architecture* (October 1986).

Kendall,Stephen, "Shell / Infill A Technical Study of A New Strategy for 2x4 House Building," *Open House International*, vol 15, no.1 (1990).

Kendall, Stephen, "Open Building for Housing," *Progressive Architecture* (November 1993).

Kendall, Stephen, "Prospects for Open

Building in the US Housing Industry," *Proceedings, First International Conference on Open Building and Structure Engineering, Southeast University, Nanjing* (PRC, 1995).

Kendall, Stephen, "Europe's Matura Infill System Quickly Routes Utilities for Custom Remodeling," *Automated Builder* (May 1996).

Kendall, Stephen, "A New Multifamily Housing Paradigm," *Urban land* (November 1996).

Kendall, Stephen, "Open Building: An Approach to Sustainable Architecture," *Journal of Urban Technology* (December 1999).

Kendall, Stephen, "Toward Open Building: Practical Developments in Europe," *Open House International*, vol 25, no.4. (2000, pp 84-94).

Kendall, Stephen, and Jonathan Teicher: Residential Open Building, 301 p., Spon, London and New York, 2000, ISBN 0-419-23830-1

Kendall, Stephen, "Product Bundling or Kitting: Balancing Efficiency and Variety for the Market," National Consortium of Housing Research Centers Session at the NAHB Builders Show, *Proceedings: Profit and Opportunity Beyond Traditional Building Practices*, Michigan State University Urban Affairs Program (January 2003, pp 7-21).

Kendall, Stephen, "An Open Building Strategy for Converting Obsolete Office Buildings to Residential Uses," *Proceedings, 11th Annual Conference on Lean Construction* (Blacksburg, VA., 2003, pp 207-218).

Kendall, Stephen, "Making Accommodating Residential Form: International Developments toward an Open Architecture," *Proceedings 23rd Annual Conference of the International Association of Housing Science* (Montreal, June 2003). (CD)

Kendall, Stephen, "An Open Building Strategy for Achieving Dwelling Unit Autonomyin Multi-unit Housing," *Housing and Society*, Vol 31, No.1 (2004, pp. 89-99).

Proveniers, Ir. Adri, Prof. dr. Helga Fassbinder, *New Wave in Building, a flexible way of design, construction and real estate management* (Van Gorcum, Assen / Maastricht: Eindhoven University of technology, 72p.).

Tiuri, Ulpu, Markku Hedman, *Developments Towards Open Building in Finland* (Helsinki University of Technology, Department of Architecture, 1998, 65p.).

Ulpu Tiuri, "Open Building - Housing for Real People," *Arkkitehti* (Finland, 3-1998, p22-60).

Vreedenburgh, Eric (ed), *Entangled Building* (The Netherlands: Werkgroep OBOM TU Delf, 1992).

Werf, Frans van der, *Open Ontwerpen*, ISBN 90-6450-172-6, (Uitgeverij 010, Rotterdam 1993, 179p.).

Appendix 3 Notes on Attribution and Sources

Cover drawing : Yumi Kendall

Fig 1-7 : Drawn by Zhong Hong

Fig 8 : Matura Netherlends BV

Fig 9: Age van Randen / OBOM/ TUDelft, The Netherlands

Fig 10-11 : Drawn by Zhong Hong

Fig 12: Photo by Stephen Kendall

Fig 13-30 : Drawn by Zhong Hong

Fig 31-32: Eaton - Holec, BV

Fig 33-38: Drawn by Zhong Hong

www.ingramcontent.com/pod-product-compliance
Ingram Content Group UK Ltd.
Pitfield, Milton Keynes, MK11 3LW, UK
UKHW041844190726
13854UKWH00002B/711

9 781412 094245